250 Chinese Words to Get You Around Beijing

主编　李杰群　李杰明

编著　李杰群　李杰明　向艺芬　马骏鹰

翻译　韩芙芸

插图　郝志云

Printed in China

华语教学出版社

SINOLINGUA

First Edition 2005

ISBN 7-80200-099-8

Copyright 2005 by Sinolingua

Published by Sinolingua

24 Baiwanzhuang Road, Beijing 100037, China

Tel: (86) 10-68995871/68326333

Fax: (86) 10-68326333

http://www. sinolingua. com. cn

E-mail: hyjx@sinolingua. com. cn

Printed by Beijing Foreign Languages Printing House

Distributed by China International

Book Trading Corporation

35 Chegongzhuang Xilu, P. O. Box 399

Beijing 100044, China

Printed in the People's Republic of China

编写说明

2008 年的奥运会是中国与世界对话的机会。但是,用什么语言进行对话呢? 让中国人都说英语? 这一是比较难;二是外国人也不都说英语。反过来想,让外国人都说汉语?

看起来这是把麻烦推给了外国人,其实不是。因为,与其让中国人学会全世界的无数种语言,不如让外国人只尝试一种——汉语!

汉语不难,就是字多。

中华书局和中国友谊出版公司 1994 年联合出版的《中华字海》,收 86000 多字,这是历代积累的总字数。就是现代汉字,也大约有 10000 多个(苏培成《现代汉字学纲要》,北京大学出版社,2001)。这些数字不仅对外国人是天文,就连中国人自己也受不了! 于是,从既方便外国人又改革自己的愿望出发,我们选了近 250 个汉字(汉字记录的是汉语中的语素或词),组成 168 组对话,希望可以达到在日常生活中完成交际的目的。

您相信吗? 掌握约 250 个汉字就能够在北京,甚至在中国旅游生活。我们这本书把这个神话变成了现实。这可不是耸人听闻,是有理论根据的。根据《现代汉语字频统计表》显示,最高频 500 字的覆盖率大约是 80%,该表统计的是书面材料,与日常口语还是有差异的。对于初到北京的外国人来说掌握 200 多个汉字就够用了。

本书共分为"吃喝、住宿、交通、玩乐、买东西、看病、求助"七大类,每类中所属的对话按交际场景顺序排列。对话一般由 10 个以下汉字组成。

每组对话除注汉语拼音、英文翻译外,大多还附有"类似说法、反义、幽默、联想、贴心提示"等内容,其中"联想"主要是列出一些相关的词语，"贴心提示"则是想起到一点点旅游指南的作用。有大部分的对话附了插图。

吹点牛说吧，外国朋友拿着我们这本书和一张北京地图，就可以在北京畅通无阻！

本书由李杰群、李杰明、向艺芬、马骏鹰编写，韩芙芸翻译，郝志云插图。

特别感谢华语教学出版社的韩晖女士在成书过程中的鼎力相助！

限于水平，有不妥之处，望读者赐教。联系方式：

地址　100081　北京海淀区皂君庙甲 4 号　北京广播电视大学中文系

电话　010-62113007　62148320　62113685

传真　010-62148279

E-mail：lijq@mail. btvu. org

编著者
2005 年 5 月
于北京西郊红果园

A Note from the Compilers

The 2008 Olympics Games is a chance for China to converse with the whole world. But what language will we use? Could we teach Chinese people to speak English? That would be a fairly difficult thing to do, and even if we could, we know that not all foreigners visiting China understand English. So we asked, why not approach the problem from the other direction, let foreigners speak Chinese? It might appear that we are simply passing the burden of language learning on to foreigners, but that is not our intent. We believe it would be better to let foreigners learn one language ——Chinese——than to try to teach Chinese people to speak many different foreign languages.

Foreigners might think that Chinese is difficult because it has too many characters.

The dictionary *Zhonghua Zihai* (Encyclopedic Dictionary of Chinese Characters) jointly published by Zhonghua Book Company and China Friendship Publishing Corporation contains 86,000 Chinese characters which have accumulated over the long history of the Chinese language. If we consider only modern Chinese characters, there are still more than 10,000 according to the *Compendium of Modern Chinese Characters* by Su Peicheng published by Peking University Press in 2001. This number is like an astronomical figure even to Chinese people, let alone foreigners! So we selected around 250 Chinese characters to make up the 168 dialogues in this book to facilitate foreigners' study as well as simplify our own language. It is our hope that these characters will act as a bridge for foreigners so that they can speak with Chinese people in their daily life.

You might find it difficult to believe that you can live in Beijing or even travel around China after grasping less than 250 Chinese words. Using this book, that dream is within your reach. This claim is not an exaggeration, it is based on the study of the *Statistics of Modern Chinese Character Frequency* which shows that the most frequently used 500 characters cover about 80% of daily language. Moreover, these statistics are based on written materials which are more difficult to master than spoken language. For speaking, roughly 200 Chinese characters will surely be enough for foreigners who have just arrived in Beijing.

This book is divided into seven chapters including eating and drinking, accommodation, transportation, entertainment, shopping, seeing a doctor and asking for help. The relevant dialogues comprising three to five Chinese characters will be provided as they might occur in their particular situation in each chapter.

To each dialogue will be attached Similar Expressions, Antonyms, Humor, Associations, Tips plus *Pinyin* and English annotation. Most of the dialogues are illustrated. Under the Association column are some relevant words and Tips which may help guide your visit.

Believe it, foreigners can deal with every occasion and get around Beijing with only this book and a map of the city!

This book has been compiled by Li Jiequn, Li Jieming, Xiang Yifen, Ma Junying, translated by Han Fuyun and illustrated by Hao Zhiyun.

Our special thanks go to Ms. Han Hui of Sinolingua who helped us greatly!

Comments and suggestions are welcome. You may contact us at:

Chinese Department
Beijing Radio & Television University
A4 Zaojunmiao Street, Haidian District
Beijing 100081
China
Telephone: 010-62113007   62148320   62113685
Fax: 010-62148279
E-mail: lijq@mail. btvu. org

May 2005
Hawthorn Orchard, West Suburb, Beijing

作者简介

李杰群,四川成都人,1948 年生。1982 年毕业于首都师范大学中文系。现任北京广播电视大学中文系教授。从事古代汉语、言语交际教学与研究工作。主要论著有:《汉语流行口语》《〈商君书〉虚词研究》《古代汉语》《非言语交际概论》《公共关系实用语言》《连词"则"的起源和发展》《"甚"的词性演变》《上古汉语程度副词考辨》《〈马氏文通〉的作者不容混淆》《〈孟子〉总括副词辨析》等。

李杰明,四川成都人,1953 年生。1984 年毕业于北京大学图书馆系。1986 年毕业于北京高等教育自学考试中文系。现任北京舞蹈学院学报、院报编辑,首都师范大学、北京理工大学、北京工业大学对外汉语教学兼职教师。从事文化艺术、对外汉语教学与研究工作。主要论著有:《汉语流行口语》《文明服务语言艺术》《唐宋八大家鉴赏辞典》《中国文学名著故事大观》《关于视听说课》等。

向艺芬,江西九江人,1972 年生。2001 年毕业于南昌大学中文系,文学硕士。现任中央广播电视大学讲师。从事比较文学及教学管理的工作与研究。主要论著有:《论 T．S．艾略特荒原的产生》《妇女文学和女权文化》等。

马骏鹰,河北张家口人,1973 年生。2002 年毕业于浙江师范大学中文系,文学硕士。现任北京广播电视大学讲师。从事中国古代文学、北京历史文化教学与研究工作。主要论著有:《王逸〈渔父章句〉校记》《读韩愈〈答刘秀才论史书〉札记》《读〈史记·东越列传〉》《流行汉语 200 句》等。

Introductions of the Authors

1. Li Jiequn was born in 1948 in Chengdu, Sichuan Province. He graduated from the Chinese Language Department of Capital Normal University in 1982. He is currently a professor in the Chinese Language Department of Beijing Radio and Television University, studying ancient Chinese, language communication teaching and research. His main works are *Popular Spoken Chinese*, *Studies on Function Words in Shangjunshu*, *Ancient Chinese*, *An Outline of Non-language Communications*, *Practical Words for Public Relations*, *The Origin and Development of Conjunction Word Ze*, *Evolution of Shen's Part of Speech*, *Research in Degree Adverb of Primitive Chinese*, *The Author of Mashiwentong can not be Confused*, *Research on Adverbs used in Mencius*.

2. Liu Jieming was born in 1953 in Chengdu, Sichuan Province. He graduated from the Library Department of Peking University in 1984 and in 1986 he passed the Chinese Language Department of Beijing Higher Education Self-study Exam. He is currently an editor of Beijing Dance College Journal and a part-time instructor of teaching Chinese as a foreign language in Capital Normal University, Beijing Institute of Technology, and the Beijing University of Technology. He is engaged in research on culture and the arts, and teaching Chinese as a foreign language. His main works include *Popular Spoken Chinese*, *The Art of Language in Civilized Service*, *Appreciation Dictionary of Eight Litterateurs in the Tang*

and Song Dynasties, *Stories from Famous Chinese Novels*, *On Visual*, *Listening and Speaking Courses*.

3. Xiang Yifen was born in 1972 in Jiujiang, Jiangxi Province. She graduated from the Chinese Language Department of Nanchang University in 2001 with a Master of Arts degree. She is currently a lecturer at China Central Radio and TV University, engaged in research and teaching in comparative literature and teaching management. Her main works are *On Arising of the Waste Land by T. S. Elliot*, *Women Literature* and *Feminism Culture*.

4. Ma Junying was born in 1973 in Zhangjiakou, Hebei Province. He graduated from the Chinese Language Department of Zhejiang Normal University in 2002 with a Master of Arts degree. He is currently a lecturer at Beijing Radio and TV Univeristy, engaged in research and teaching in ancient Chinese literature, history and culture of Beijing. His main works include *Notes on Proofreading Fishman's Words by Wang Yi*, *Reading Notes on Answering Scholar Liu's Article about History Books by Han Yu*, *Reading Notes of Dongyue Biography in Records of the Historian*, 200 *Popular Chinese Sentences*.

目 录
Contents

X

06 看病 Seeing a Doctor /302

01 吃 喝
chī hē **Eating and Drinking**

1 吃饭去!
Chīfàn qù!
Time to eat!

对话 Dialogue

A:吃饭去!
Chīfàn qù! Time to eat!
B:走!
Zǒu! Let's go!

类似说法 Similar Expressions

饿了。/肚子咕咕叫了。 I am hungry. / My stomach keeps rumbling.

反义 Antonym

吃饭去! —— 不想吃。 Time to eat! I dont't want to eat.

幽默 Humor

该喂脑袋了。/修五脏庙。 Time to feed. / I am so hungry I could eat a horse!

联想 Association

该做饭了! /该买菜了! /饭卡放哪儿了? Time to cook! / Time to buy some groceries! / Where is the meal card?

《孟子·告子上》中说:"食色,性也。" 意思是说,饮食男女,这是人的本性。自古以来中国人就非常重视饮食,中国的饮食文化丰富多彩。"吃了吗,您呢?"也曾经是流行了几十年的见面问候语。希望您来到中国首先要吃好喝好,品尝各种风味佳肴。

"To enjoy food and sex is in human nature," according to Mencius. This means that it is natural for people to eat food and have sex. Chinese people have historically attached great importance to food and have created a variety of cuisines. "Have you eaten yet?" was once a popular greeting. We hope you eat and drink well, tasting the different cuisines in China.

2 吃快餐吗？
Chī kuàicān ma?
Do you prefer fast food?

对话 Dialogue

A:吃快餐吗？
　Chī kuàicān ma?　Do you prefer fast food?
B:不吃。
　Bù chī.　No，I do not.

类似说法 Similar Expressions

吃三明治吗？　Do you want a sandwich?

反义 Antonym

快餐——正餐　fast food——regular meal

幽默 Humor

狼吞虎咽。　Eat like a wolf.

联想 Association

麦当劳/肯德基/牛肉面/饺子/方便面
McDonald's/Kentucky Fried Chicken/beef noodles/
jiaozi/instant noodles

　　西式快餐店有必胜客、肯德基、赛百味等；日式快餐店有面爱面、吉野家；中式快餐店有老上海城隍庙小吃、成都小吃等。您可以根据您的口味挑选。

Western fast food includes Pizza Hut, Kentucky Fried Chicken, Subway and etc.; Japanese fast food includes Mian Ai Mian and Yoshinoya; Chinese fast food includes Old Shanghai Chenghuangmiao Snacks, Chengdu Snacks and so on. You may choose according to your own taste.

3

海鲜怎么样？
Hǎixiān zěnmeyàng?
What about seafood?

对话 Dialogue

A:海鲜怎么样？
Hǎixiān zěnmeyàng?　What about seafood?

B:海鲜太贵。
Hǎixiān tài guì.　It is too expensive.

类似说法 Similar Expressions

海鲜不实惠。/吃海鲜太麻烦。　Seafood is not worth the
price. / It is too difficult to eat seafood.

反义 Antonym

海鲜——死鱼　fresh seafood——dead fish

幽默 Humor

我吃那玩意儿闹肚子。/我吃海鲜怎么也吃不饱。
I always get diarrhea after eating seafood. / Seafood is not
filling.

联想 Association

深海鱼/大龙虾/大螃蟹/鲍鱼/扇贝
deep sea fish/big lobster/big crab/abalone/scallop

　　如果吃海鲜就不要怕花钱，便宜的不新鲜，吃了会闹肚子。

　　Although seafood is expensive, we do not recommend that you choose low-end restaurants for seafood. Seafood that is not fresh may cause diarrhea.

吃西餐吗?
Chī xīcān ma?
Would you like to eat western foods?

对话 Dialogue

A：吃西餐吗？

　　Chī xīcān ma?　Would you like to eat western foods?

B：不想吃。

　　Bù xiǎng chī.　No, thank you.

类似说法 Similar Expressions

去西餐厅？　Western restaurant?

反义 Antonym

西餐——中餐　Western food——Chinese food

幽默 Humor

你请客我就去。　I'll go if you treat me.

联想 Association

马克希姆餐厅/季诺/莫斯科餐厅/星期五餐厅
Maxim's/ Gino/ Moscow Restaurant/ Friday's

北京的西餐厅很多,法式、意大利式、俄式、美式都有。使馆区、大学区、三里屯、后海等地比较集中。

There are many western restaurants in Beijing which serve French, Italian, Russian and American styles. These restaurants are mostly around districts near embassies, universities, Sanlidun and Houhai.

想吃烧烤。
Xiǎng chī shāokǎo.
I am thinking of barbecue.

对话 Dialogue

A：想吃烧烤。

　　Xiǎng chī shāokǎo.　I am thinking of barbecue!

B：烧烤上火。

　　Shāokǎo shànghuǒ.　Barbecue may be hard on your health.

类似说法 Similar Expressions

韩国烧烤/烤牛肉　Korean barbecue/roast beef

反义 Antonym

烧烤——清蒸　roast——steam

幽默 Humor

烟熏火燎。　It smokes and burns.

联想 Association

煮/煎/炸/烹　cook/fry/deepfry/boil

贴心提示 Tips

　　中国菜讲究的是炒；西餐喜欢烤。可是目前北京特别流行的是韩国烧烤，满街都是韩国烧烤店，而且座无虚席。尽管有权威机构公布了烧烤对健康不利，但是人们还是蜂拥而至。

Chinese dishes tend to be done by sautéing or stir frying while western dishes are done by roasting. Currently Korean barbecue is popular in Beijing. Korean restaurants are everywhere and all are crowded with customers. Health authorities have warned that too much barbecue is not good for your health, but people just ignore this advice.

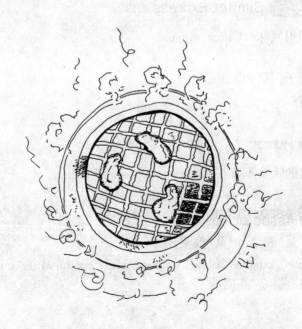

6 川菜人多。
Chuān cài rén duō.
It is too crowded in Sichuan cuisine restaurants.

对话 Dialogue

A：吃川菜吗？

Chī chuāncài ma?　What do you think of Sichuan cuisine?

B：川菜人多。

Chuāncài rén duō.　It is too crowded in Sichuan restaurants.

类似说法 Similar Expressions

四川风味　Chuan cuisine

反义 Antonym

多——少　crowded——empty

幽默 Humor

我的舌头不在了。　I cannot feel my tongue.

联想 Association

粤菜/湘菜/沪菜/鲁菜/潮州菜
Yue cuisine/Xiang cuisine/Hu cuisine/Lu cuisine/Chaozhou cuisine

中国的四大菜系是川(四川)、鲁(山东)、粤(广东)、苏(江苏)。川菜麻辣。粤菜甜软,以海鲜为主。其他风味多多,胃口好的话,应逐一品尝。

The four most famous cuisines in China are Chuan (Sichuan Province), Lu (Shangdong Province), Yue (Guangdong Province) and Su (Jiangsu Province). The hot and spicy cuisine of Sichuan is at one extreme, and the sweet and soft Yue cuisine at the other, with a lot of seafood. There are other flavours besides these. If you have a good appetite, you may try as many as you can.

烤鸭太油！
Kǎoyā tài yóu!
Roast duck is too greasy!

对话 Dialogue

A:烤鸭行吗？
Kǎoyā xíng ma?　What about Roast Beijing Duck?
B:烤鸭太油！
Kǎoyā tài yóu!　It is too greasy!

类似说法 Similar Expressions

太腻/油太多　too greasy/ too much oil

反义 Antonym

油——清爽　greasy——lite

联想 Association

卷饼/大葱/甜面酱/鸭汤/全鸭宴/卤鸭肝
thin cake /scallion/Peking Duck sauce/duck-bone soup/
duck banquet/pot-stewed duck liver

　　北京烤鸭真的非常有名,没吃过的人无论如何也得尝一口。当然要去正宗的全聚德烤鸭店。正像俗话说的"不到长城非好汉,不吃烤鸭真遗憾"。

Roast Beijing Duck is so famous that everyone should try it. We recommend you to go to the authentic Quan Ju De Restaurant. There is a saying to the effect that you will not become a hero until you visit the Great Wall, and you will regret it if you do not eat Roast Beijing Duck .

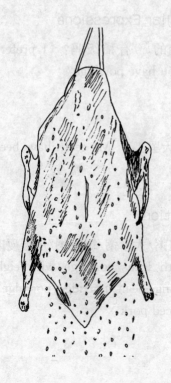

8

我想喝粥。
Wǒ xiǎng hē zhōu.
I'd like porridge.

对话 Dialogue

A：你想吃什么？
　Nǐ xiǎng chī shénme?　Do you have anything in mind?
B：我想喝粥。
　Wǒ xiǎng hē zhōu.　I'd like porridge.

类似说法 Similar Expressions

我想喝点稀的。/有稀饭吗？　I prefer something with soup. /Do you have porridge?

幽默 Humor

我的牙这两天罢工。　My teeth have been on strike these days.

联想 Association

莲子粥/八宝粥/大米粥/绿豆粥/皮蛋瘦肉粥
porridge with lotus/porridge with eight treasures/rice porridge/mung bean porridge/porridge with perserved egg and minced pork

16

中国以前一般在三种时候喝粥，一是早上，一是晚上，一是病了。中国人认为粥便于消化，有滋补作用。现在习惯有点变了，街上的粥店也开始多起来，有几十种粥供您选择。很多人中午也去喝粥。目前比较好的是宏状元粥店，有好多家连锁店。

In the past Chinese people would only have porridge in the morning or evening or when they were sick, thinking that porridge is easy to digest and nourishing. This idea is changing. There are many porridge restaurants on the streets now selling dozens of different flavours. Many people also go to porridge restaurants at lunchtime. At present Hong Zhuang Yuan Porridge Restaurant is the best chain of restaurants of this type.

9 几位?
Jǐ wèi?
How many people?

对话 Dialogue

A: 几位?
　　Jǐ wèi?　How many people?
B: 两位。
　　Liǎng wèi.　Two.

类似说法 Similar Expressions

欢迎光临！/您来了！　Welcome! /How do you do!

联想 Association

几位先生/几位小姐/几位朋友
how many gentlemen/how many ladies/how many friends

这是饭馆门口服务生的常用招呼语，他好根据顾客人数安排桌位。您可以在回答的同时做出手势，表示强调。

This is the most commonly used greeting by the host or hostess at the door. They arrange the table according to the number of guests. You may emphasize your answer with a gesture.

10 坐那儿行吗？
Zuò nàr xíng ma?
How about sitting there?

对话 Dialogue

　A:请坐这边。

　　Qǐng zuò zhèbiān.　Sit here please.

　B:坐那儿行吗？

　　Zuò nàr xíng ma?　How about sitting there?

类似说法 Similar Expressions

我想坐那张桌子。/我喜欢靠窗户坐。 I want to switch
to that table. /I prefer window seat.

反义 Antonym

坐——站　sit——stand

联想 Association

站这儿吧！/躺这儿吧！ Stand here! /Lie here!

　　坐哪儿吃是个很重要的问题,也是矛盾,因为人多的饭馆才火,饭菜也可能好吃。解决的办法是错开高峰期,这样既能吃到好饭菜,又不至于受拥挤。

To choose good seats in a restaurant matters greatly. But generally restaurants with more people serve better food. You'd better stagger the rush hour to enjoy a good meal while avoiding the crowd.

11

点菜吗?
Diǎn cài ma?
Are you ready to order?

对话 Dialogue

A: 点菜吗?

　Diǎn cài ma?　Are you ready to order?

B: 我先看看。

　Wǒ xiān kànkan.　Let me look at the menu first.

类似说法 Similar Expressions

吃点什么? /您先看看菜单。　What would you like to order? /Have a look at the menu first.

反义 Antonym

点菜——随便上　order——anything will do.

幽默 Humor

全都尝尝吧!　Let me taste all the dishes!

联想 Association

点歌/点将/点名/点播　select a song/assign somebody to a task/call the roll/ request broadcasting programme

　　有的服务员会给你推荐很贵的菜,有的服务员不会推荐菜,所以你最好听去吃过的人介绍某菜,当然有时候乱点一道也可能很不错,那就看你的运气了。

Some waiters will recommend expensive dishes whereas some will not give any recommendation. It is better to ask someone who has been to the restaurant before to recommend some dishes. You can also choose on your own and probably get a good result. That might, however, depend on your luck.

你想吃什么?
Nǐ xiǎng chī shénme?
Do you have something in mind?

对话 Dialogue

A:你想吃什么?
　Nǐ xiǎng chī shénme?　Do you have something in
　mind?
B:随便。
　Suíbiàn.　Anything will do.

类似说法 Similar Expressions

喜欢吃什么?　What would you prefer?

反义 Antonym

吃——喝　eat——drink

幽默 Humor

什么都想吃。　I'll eat anything.

联想 Association

想买点儿什么/想喝点儿什么/想玩点儿什么
What do you want to buy? / What do you want to
drink? / What do you want to play?

在中国，一般是主人(付账的人)点菜，但又一定要问客人的意思。客人呢，最好听主人的意思，因为主人大多是有所准备的。

In China the host usually orders the dishes, but he will ask the guests what they want first. Guests should follow the host's choice because the host knows the restaurant and is well prepared to choose.

13 喝什么茶?
Hē shénme chá?
What sort of tea would you like to drink?

对话 Dialogue

A: 喝什么茶?

Hē shénme chá?　What sort of tea would you like to drink?

B: 是免费的吗?

Shì miǎnfèi de ma?　Is it free?

类似说法 Similar Expressions

喝点什么? /要什么酒水?　Do you want something to drink? / What would you like to drink?

反义 Antonym

茶——白水　tea——water

幽默 Humor

是茶就行。　Any kind of tea will do.

联想 Association

可口可乐/雪碧/果汁/牛奶/矿泉水　Coca Cola/ Sprite/ juice/milk/mineral water

去饭馆吃饭，一般都要点佐餐的饮料，许多中国人喜欢喝茶，大众化的餐馆一般都供应免费茶。

We usually order some drinks when dining out. Chinese prefer tea, which is usually provided free in the more popular restaurants.

14

没有不要钱的。

Méiyǒu búyào qián de.

There is no free tea. (Nothing is free)

对话 Dialogue

A:没有不要钱的。

　Méiyǒu búyào qián de.　There is no free tea.

B:那就白开水。

　Nà jiù bái kāi shuǐ.　Just hot water please.

类似说法 Similar Expressions

都是要钱的。/没有免费的。/本店没有。　Everything will be included in the bill. / There is no free tea. / We don't have that.

反义 Antonym

没有——有　don't have——have

幽默 Humor

天底下没有不要钱的。　There is no free lunch.

联想 Association

茶水/矿泉水　tea/ mineral water

28

低档的饭馆,茶水免费,中高档的饭馆,茶水都要钱。饮料更是商店的 3－5 倍。因此很多人不在饭馆要酒水。

Tea is free in low-grade restaurants and is usually charged for in higher grade restaurants. The prices for drinks at a higher grade restaurant will be 3-5 times higher than in supermarkets. Therefore many people do not order drinks in restaurants.

15

服务员！点菜！
Fúwùyuán! Diǎn cài!
Waiter! We want to order please!

对话 Dialogue

A: 服务员！点菜！

Fúwùyuán! Diǎn cài!

Waiter，we want to order please!

B: 来了！

Lái le!　Coming!

类似说法 Similar Expressions

小姐/小妹/小伙子/姑娘

miss/ young sister/mate/madam

反义 Antonym

服务员——经理/领班

waiter——manager/head servant

幽默 Humor

水都喝饱了,怎么无人理睬呢? I am full from drinking the water and nobody has come to take our order.

联想 Association

拿点餐巾纸。/加点开水。 Napkin please. /More hot water please.

北京的服务质量比较好,有什么意见的话,您就对经理提出来,不必与服务员争吵。

Good services are provided in Beijing. If you are not satisfied, you may complain to the manager, so it is not necessary to quarrel with the waiter.

16

要什么酒水?
Yào shénme jiǔ shuǐ?
What would you like to drink?

对话 Dialogue

A: 要什么酒水?

Yào shénme jiǔ shuǐ?   What would you like to drink?

B: 红酒。

Hóngjiǔ.   Red wine.

类似说法 Similar Expressions

喝点什么? /需要什么饮料?   Would you like something
to drink? /What kind of drinks do you want?

反义 Antonym

要——不要   want——do not want

幽默 Humor

开车了吗?   Did you drive?

联想 Association

啤酒/小二锅头/洋酒/色酒/鸡尾酒
beer/small bottle of *Erguotou*/foreign wine/wine/cocktail

贴心提示 Tips

不少北京的男人喝56度的"二锅头",5块钱1斤装。最酷的女人也喝。

Many gentlemen in Beijing are used to drinking *Erguotou*, a hard liquor containing 56 percent alcohol. This costs 5 yuan per bottle. The coolest women also drink *Erguotou*.

33

17

干杯!
Gānbēi!
Cheers!

对话 Dialogue

A：干杯!
　　Gānbēi!　Cheers!
B：干杯!
　　Gānbēi!　Cheers!

类似说法 Similar Expressions

来一口! /喝一气儿! /端起来!　Have a mouthful! /
Drink a round! /Hold up!

反义 Antonym

干杯! ——请随意!　Cheers! ——Help yourself!

幽默 Humor

会喝酒吗?　Are you good at drinking?

联想 Association

喝着/吃着/玩儿着/唱着/跳着
drinking/eating/playing/singing/jumping

"干"是一口喝完的意思，没酒量就别跟着说。能喝就喝，不能喝就少喝或不喝，千万别因为主人的盛情而被送进医院。

"Gan" means drinking to the bottom. Don't say it when you are not good at drinking. It is not proper to be sent to the hospital due to excessive drink.

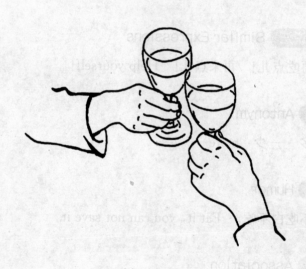

18 多吃点儿!
Duō chī diǎnr!
Eat more!

对话 Dialogue

A：多吃点儿!
　　Duō chī diǎnr!　Eat more!
B：我吃不了了!
　　Wǒ chī bu liǎo le!　I am full.

类似说法 Similar Expressions

再吃点儿! /再来点儿!　Help yourself!

反义 Antonym

多——少　more——less

幽默 Humor

不吃白不吃。　Eat it, you can not save it.

联想 Association

多喝点儿! /多玩儿会儿! /多呆会儿!
Drink more! /Have fun! /Stay longer!

贴心提示 Tips

如果主人过分热情,您可以不必认真;吃饱了,就不用再吃了。

A good Chinese host may be overwhelming, you do not have to eat more if you are full no matter how much they might encourage you. Enough is enough.

19 服务员，买单。
Fúwùyuán, mǎi dān.
Waiter, bill please!

对话 Dialogue

A: 服务员，买单。
Fúwùyuán, mǎi dān. Waiter, bill please.

B: 我来我来。
Wǒ lái wǒ lái. It's on me.

类似说法 Similar Expressions

结账/算账/打单/付账 pay the bill/cast the account/ print the bill/settle the account

反义 Antonym

买单——白吃 pay the bill——be treated

幽默 Humor

我去洗手间了。/我忘带钱了。 I have to go to the restroom. / I forgot to bring money with me.

联想 Association

核对/多退少补 check/ refund for any overpayment or deficiency

比较传统的中国人，习惯抢着付钱，表示热情、大方、够朋友。这时候，您也可以表示一下，但是，别只顾争着付钱，账单到手后别忘了认真核对一下。

现在也有 AA 制的。

It is a tradition that Chinese will rush to pay the bill when dining out with friends or relatives. They think this is a way to show their generosity and kindness. You are advised to do the same. But do not forget to check the bill when paying.

It is also now popular to go Dutch.

20

您这是 65 块。
Nín zhè shì liùshíwǔ kuài.
The total is 65 yuan.

对话 Dialogue

A: 您这是 65 块。

Nín zhè shì liùshíwǔ kuài. The total is 65 yuan.

B: 给您。

Gěi nín. Here it is.

类似说法 Similar Expressions

您的消费是 65 元。/ 这是找您的钱。

The total price is 65 yuan. / Here is your change.

反义 Antonym

您今天的消费是 65 元——老板说免您的单。

You spent 65 yuan today. ——Our boss treats you.

贴心提示 Tips

在中国一般不讲给小费,该付多少付多少。不用说"别找了"那种话,说了反而不好。另外,别忘了要正式发票,说不定你可以刮出一笔大奖金呢!

It is unusual in China to pay a tip. So do not say "Keep the change". Do not forget to ask for a formal invoice because it often contains a lottery and you may win money after scratching the covered area on it!

21

请您打包。
Qǐng nín dǎ bāo.
Please wrap this to take away.

对话 Dialogue

A:请您打包。
　Qǐng nín dǎ bāo.　Please wrap this to take away.
B:好。
　Hǎo.　Okay.

类似说法 Similar Expressions

这些剩菜要带走。/装盒吧。/吃不了兜着走。
Take these leftover dishes home. / Put these into a box. /
Take all leftover food home.

反义 Antonym

打包。——不要了。　take away——won't take away

幽默 Humor

我那猫还饿着呢。　My cat is still hungry.

联想 Association

节约/俭朴/会过日子/不大手大脚
economical/thrifty/not wasteful/not extravagant

42

把在饭店没吃完的东西拿回家下顿再吃是个好习惯，而要很多菜吃不了应该受到批评。

It is a good habit to take the leftover food home. It does not make any sense to order too many dishes just to show your wealth.

住 宿
zhù sù **Accommodation**

22
住哪儿好？
Zhù nǎr hǎo?
Where is better to live?

对话 Dialogue

A:住哪儿好？
Zhù nǎr hǎo? Where is better to live?
B:住大学好。
Zhù dàxué hǎo. Living in universities is better.

类似说法 Similar Expressions

住哪儿又安全又便宜？ Where is safer and cheaper?

反义 Antonym

好——坏 good——bad

幽默 Humor

住车站好,不用花钱。 It is free to live in the railway station.

联想 Association

单位招待所/星级宾馆/国营旅馆/私人小旅馆
inn attached to a company/star hotel/state-owned hotel/
private inn

44

　　大城市可住宿的地方很多，住在大学里比较安全，价钱又不贵。北京的大学比较集中在西北部的学院路和中关村大街一带，东南部只有中国传媒大学、第二外国语大学、首都经贸大学等几所。详细地址还得看地图。市内的正规宾馆价位都比较高，私人小旅馆注意看有没有营业执照，无论住哪家旅馆，贵重物品都请您随身带好。

There are many places for your choice of accommodation. Hotels in universities are safer and cheaper. You may check the map to find the locations of all universities. State-owned hotels are more expensive. If you choose to stay in private inns, please make sure they are licensed.

23

有房间吗？
Yǒu fángjiān ma?
Do you have any vacancies?

对话 Dialogue

A:有房间吗？
　　Yǒu fángjiān ma?　Do you have any vacancies?
B:有两人间。
　　Yǒu liǎng rén jiān.　We have double rooms.

类似说法 Similar Expressions

有地儿住吗？　Do you have rooms to rent?

幽默 Humor

门庭若市。　There are too many visitors here, it looks like a market.

联想 Association

单人间/标准二人间/普通二人间
single room/standard double room/ordinary double room

如果是旅游高峰时期,各旅馆住宿都比较紧张,可以提前请熟人或打电话预定好房间。

As hotels are often full during the peak tourist season, you may ask friends to telephone ahead or call yourself to make reservations.

24

多少钱一天？
Duōshǎo qián yì tiān?
What is the price per night?

对话 Dialogue

A：多少钱一天？
Duōshǎo qián yì tiān?　What is the price per night?
B：一天 120。
Yì tiān yìbǎi èrshí.　120 yuan per night.

类似说法 Similar Expressions

价位多少？　How much does it cost?

反义 Antonym

多——少　many——few

幽默 Humor

白天我都不在。　I do not stay during daytime.

联想 Association

200/300/400(元)

　　可以问问服务员能不能打折或优惠一点，一般住得时间长会便宜些。

　　You may ask the attendant to give you a more favorable price. They usually give a discount when you are staying longer.

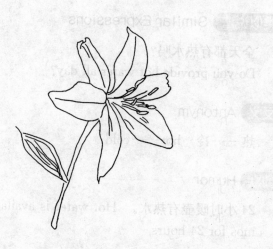

25 有热水吗?
Yǒu rè shuǐ ma?
Is hot water available?

对话 Dialogue

A：有热水吗?
　　Yǒu rè shuǐ ma?　Is hot water available?
B：24 小时有热水。
　　Èrshísì xiǎoshí yǒu rè shuǐ.　Yes，24 hours a day.

类似说法 Similar Expressions

全天都有热水吗?
Do you provide hot water all day?

反义 Antonym

热——冷　hot——cold

幽默 Humor

24 小时暖壶有热水。　Hot water is available in the thermos for 24 hours.

联想 Association

有暖气吗? /有空调吗? /有电话吗? /有洗衣机吗? /有电视吗?　Do you have central heating? /Is the room air-conditioned? / Do you have a telephone? /Do you provide laundry? /Do you have a TV in the room?

50

热水是住宿的重要条件，一般全天有热水比较方便。假如是定时供应热水，一定要在其它时间安排好事情，避免错过洗热水澡。

Hot water is a necessity. It is more convenient to find a room where hot water is available twenty-four hours a day. When hot water is only provided during certain periods of the day, proper arrangements must be made in advance in order not to miss it.

26 我要个两人间。
Wǒ yào ge liǎng rén jiān.
I'd like a double room.

对话 Dialogue

A：我要个两人间。

Wǒ yào ge liǎng rén jiān.　I'd like a double room.

B：好的。

Hǎo de.　Okay.

类似说法 Similar Expressions

我要个标准间。　I'd like a standard room.

反义 Antonym

要——不要　want——do not want

联想 Association

单人间/二人间/三人间

single room/ double room/ room with three beds

如果是单独住宿，最好一人包一个房间，这样比较安全和卫生。

If you are traveling on your own, it is better for your health and safety to book a single room.

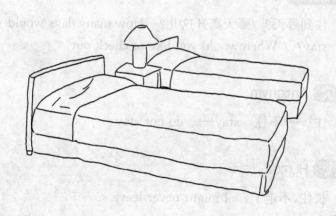

住几天?
Zhù jǐ tiān?
How long would you expect to stay?

对话 Dialogue

A: 住几天?

Zhù jǐ tiān?　How long would you expect to stay?

B: 5 天。

Wǔ tiān.　5 days.

类似说法 Similar Expressions

住到哪天? / 哪天离开这儿?　How many days would you stay? / When would you like to check out?

反义 Antonym

住——不住　stay——do not stay

幽默 Humor

长住,不走了。　I might never leave.

联想 Association

10 天/半个月/半年/1 年　10 days/half a month/half a year/one year

　　住旅馆一般都要提前告诉服务员大概住几天,如果要延期住宿,也需要提前告诉服务员。

　　It is usual to inform the attendant the length of your stay at the beginning. If you want to extend your stay, please advise them in advance.

28

请先交 500。
Qǐng xiān jiāo wǔbǎi.
Please prepay 500 yuan.

对话 Dialogue

A：请先交 500。

　　Qǐng xiān jiāo wǔbǎi.　Please prepay 500 yuan.

B：给您。

　　Gěi nín.　Here you are.

类似说法 Similar Expressions

先交 500 元押金吧，结账时多退少补。

Please pay a deposit of 500 yuan and settle the account when checking out.

反义 Antonym

先——后　before——later

幽默 Humor

押东西行吗？　Can I use some objects as a deposit?

联想 Association

押金/预订金/预收款　deposit/reservation/prepayment

56

交了押金要记得索取收据，在结账时有可能冲抵住房费。

Don't forget to ask for a confirmation slip or receipt for your deposit, this amount can be deducted from your bill.

29

请这边走。
Qǐng zhèbiān zǒu.
This way, please!

对话 Dialogue

A：请这边走。

　　Qǐng zhèbiān zǒu.　This way, please.

B：好。

　　Hǎo.　Okay.

类似说法 Similar Expressions

这边请！　Come this way please!

反义 Antonym

这边——那边　this way——that way

幽默 Humor

向左走，向右走。　Turn to the left and turn to the right.

联想 Association

在酒店里/在健身房/在茶馆/在电影院都有引路服务员。
An attendant will lead the way for you at the hotel/in the gym/at the teahouse/in a cinema.

　　跟着服务员走到你的房间,趁服务员在的时候试试门能不能打开,开门之后注意保管好房间的钥匙,休息或离开房间的时候要锁好房门。

You may follow the attendant to your room and use your key to open the door. Do not misplace the key. Remember to lock your room when leaving or having a rest.

30 代洗衣服吗？
Dài xǐ yīfu ma?
Do you accept laundry?

对话 Dialogue

A：代洗衣服吗？

Dài xǐ yīfu ma? Do you accept laundry?

B：请给服务员。

Qǐng gěi fúwùyuán. Please give it to the attendant.

类似说法 Similar Expressions

您这儿管洗衣服吗？ Do you have laundry?

幽默 Humor

我出门不洗衣服。

I never wash my clothes when going out.

联想 Association

晒衣服/换衣服

to hang wet clothes on the rack/ to change clothes

一般的宾馆都有代为客人洗衣服的业务，客房服务指南里有价格和时间等的详细说明。送洗之前，可要仔细检查衣服的口袋，避免钱或其他票据的丢失。

Usually hotels will provide laundry service. The price and schedule of the laundry service will be described in the hotel guide. Please check your pockets before giving them to the laundry to avoid any loss of money or important notes.

31

服务员,要开水!
Fúwùyuán, yào kāishuǐ!
Attendant, hot water please!

对话 Dialogue

A:服务员,要开水!
　Fúwùyuán, yào kāishuǐ! Attendant, hot water please!

B:来了。
　Lái le. Coming.

类似说法 Similar Expressions

没开水了！ Bring us some hot water please!

反义 Antonym

开水──生水 boiled water──cold water

幽默 Humor

要 100 度的水。 I mean boiling water of 100 degrees.

联想 Association

换床被子。/卫生纸没有了。/换双拖鞋。
Bring me a new quilt. /Bring some toilet paper. /Bring me a pair of slippers.

贴心提示 Tips

　　旅馆一般每天都会给顾客提供开水,有的旅馆还会提供一个电热水壶能迅速把水烧开。您假如要出去游玩,可以在走之前烧开一壶水,回来的时候就可以直接喝了。自来水目前还不能直接喝。

Hotels usually provide a thermos of boiled water as part of the room service. Some may have an electrical water heater. In this case you may boil a bottle of water before going out so as to have water to drink on your return. It is not safe to drink tap water at present.

32

服务员,电话坏了!
Fúwùyuán, diànhuà huài le!
Attendant, the telephone doesn't work!

对话 Dialogue

A:服务员,电话坏了!
　Fúwùyuán, diànhuà huài le!　Attendant, the telephone doesn't work!
B:我来看看。
　Wǒ lái kànkan.　Coming.

类似说法 Similar Expressions

电话没声了。/电话打不出去。
The telephone does not ring. / I can not dial the number.

反义 Antonym

坏——好　out of order——in good condition

幽默 Humor

我们的电话是哑巴。　Our telephones are all mute.

联想 Association

电视坏了。/空调坏了。/下水堵了。
The TV doesn't work. /The air-conditioner doesn't work. /Something is wrong with the sewer.

贴心提示 Tips

　　建议你买一台小灵通,打长途还可以拨 IP 电话。最好别用旅馆电话,因为收费太高。

It is recommended that you buy a Personal Handphone System (PHS) and make long distance calls with an IP number. Do not use the telephone in the room as it is too expensive.

33 买房还是租房?
Mǎi fáng háishì zū fáng?
Do you buy or rent a house?

对话 Dialogue

A：买房还是租房?
　　Mǎi fáng háishì zū fáng?　Do you buy or rent a house?

B：租房。
　　Zū fáng.　Rent.

类似说法 Similar Expressions

您需要什么帮助?　What kind of help do you need?

反义 Antonym

买——卖　buy——sell

联想 Association

买别墅/租公寓　to buy a villa/to rent an apartment

　　租房之前先要了解市场价格,租房价钱根据房子所在位置会差别较大。还可以上网查询房屋出租信息。

　　Before renting you may first find out the market price,which varies according to the locations. You may also go to the web to search rent information.

34

租几居的?
Zū jǐ jū de?
How many rooms to rent?

对话 Dialogue

A：租几居的?
　Zū jǐ jū de?　How many rooms to rent?
B：一居的。
　Yì jū de.　One room.

类似说法 Similar Expressions

租多大面积的? /要几居的?
How many square meters to rent? / How many rooms do
you want?

反义 Antonym

租——不租　rent——do not rent

幽默 Humor

有一居室 10 块钱 1 个月的吗?　Do you have a one-room
house for 10 yuan per month?

联想 Association

一居室/两居室/三居室　one-room apartment/two-room
apartment/three-room apartment

68

　　如果您是一个人，可以租一居室。如果有几个要好的朋友，可以几人合租一个三居室，这样比较便宜一点儿。

　　If you are living by yourself, you may rent a one-room apartment. It is cheaper to rent a three-room apartment with friends.

35

月租 1500。

Yuè zū yìqiān wǔ.

The rent is 1500 yuan per month.

（房屋中介所内，服务人员与两位顾客对话。

At the real estate agency, a staff member is talking with two customers.）

对话 Dialogue

A:月租 1500。

　　Yuè zū yìqiān wǔ.　The rent is 1500 yuan per month.

B:行，我先租一年。

　　Xíng, wǒ xiān zū yì nián.　Okay.　I want to rent for a year first.

类似说法 Similar Expressions

一个月 1500 块人民币。　It costs 1500 yuan per month.

反义 Antonym

租——不租　rent——do not rent

幽默 Humor

没钱可以住车站。　Without money you can live in the railway station.

联想 Association

日租/年租　daily rent/yearly rent

在大城市就要做好租房贵的准备,根据住的时间长短和生活或工作的需求尽可能选择性价比高的位置租房,住的时间短可以租档次较高的房子,倘若住的时间很长,就可以考虑租相对便宜、生活很方便、出行也不困难的房子。

In big cities, rent is higher. It is better to rent a house in a good location, considering the convience for the length of your stay and what you intend to do. For a short stay you may rent an upper class apartment. If you are to stay longer, you may consider renting a less expensive one.

36

先交半年房租。
Xiān jiāo bàn nián fángzū.
Please prepay rent for half a year.

对话 Dialogue

A: 先交半年房租。

　　Xiān jiāo bàn nián fángzū. Please prepay rent for half a year.

B: 好的。

　　Hǎo de. All right.

类似说法 Similar Expressions

房租半年一交。 To pay rent for every half a year.

反义 Antonym

先——后 before——later

幽默 Humor

交了之后保证不退。 Please be assured that we shall never return your prepayment.

联想 Association

三月一交/半年一交/一年一交

to pay every three months/to pay every half a year/to pay yearly.

交房租之前必须签好合同,有时盲目地交了房租可能会上当受骗。

It is necessary to sign a contract before paying the rent. If not, you will probably be cheated.

37

有 500 一个月的吗?
Yǒu wǔbǎi yí gè yuè de ma?
Do you have any houses for 500 yuan?

对话 Dialogue

A:有 500 一个月的吗?

Yǒu wǔbǎi yí gè yuè de ma?　Do you have any house for 500 yuan?

B:有平房。

Yǒu píng fáng.　Yes, it is a ranch house.

类似说法 Similar Expressions

我要租 500 块钱一个月的房子。　I'd like to rent a house for 500 yuan a month.

反义 Antonym

平房——楼房　bungalow——multi-story building

幽默 Humor

没钱也不能没房住。　One can live without money but can not live without a house.

联想 Association

地下室/合租房　basement/joint-rent house

74

无论是住平房还是地下室，都必须注意周围的环境。环境差，价钱再便宜都不能要。

No matter whether it is a bungalow or basement, the environment is important. Never choose a cheap house with a bad environment.

38 多少平米?
Duōshǎo píngmǐ?
How many square meters?

对话 Dialogue

A: 多少平米?
Duōshǎo píngmǐ? How many square meters?
B: 15 平米。
Shíwǔ píngmǐ. 15 square meters.

类似说法 Similar Expressions

多大面积? What is the area?

反义 Antonym

多——少 many——few

幽默 Humor

只够站着睡觉的地儿。 There is only enough standing
room to sleep.

联想 Association

卫生间多大? /厨房几平米? /是正方形的吗?
How big is the restroom? / How many square meters is
the kitchen? / Is it square?

15 平米足够短时期内两人居住,房子太大也是浪费空间。但是咨询的时候还需问清是建筑面积还是实际使用面积,有的房子两者相差很大,可能达不到您的要求。

A house of 15 square meters is enough for two people to stay for a short period. Please note to ask whether it refers to floor space or just internal space.

39

地下室最便宜。
Dìxiàshì zuì piányi.
The basement is the cheapest.

A:最便宜的是什么房？
Zuì piányi de shì shénme fáng?
Which is the cheapest?
B:地下室最便宜。
Dìxiàshì zuì piányi. The basement is the cheapest.

类似说法 Similar Expressions

最便宜的是地下室。 The cheapest is the basement.

反义 Antonym

地下——地上 under the ground——above the ground

幽默 Humor

没想到提前住到地下了。 I didn't expect to live underground before I died.

联想 Association

平房/筒子楼/板楼/塔楼
ranch house/office building/ narrow building/ tower building

地下室的空气不流通,而且常年都没有太阳的照射,不利因素太多,所以尽量不要租地下室。当然短期住还是可以的。

A basement apartment may not have adequate air circulation and it gets no sunshine all year long. Thus it is better not to rent a basement apartment. It can certainly be rented for very short period.

40 买房的人多吗?
Mǎi fáng de rén duō ma?
Are there many people who want to buy houses?

对话 Dialogue

A: 买房的人多吗?
Mǎi fáng de rén duō ma?　Are there many people who want to buy houses?

B: 多。
Duō.　Yes.

类似说法 Similar Expressions

大部分人都买房了。　Most people buy their own houses.

幽默 Humor

房虫。　Termites

联想 Association

打电话号码 114 查询。/上中介所查询。/上网查询。
To dial 114 to make inquiries/to inquire the agency/to check the information on the internet

为确保消息来源可靠,尽可能上正规的中介公司买房,还可以上售楼处直接和售楼人员面谈。

To ensure credible information, you'd better either purchase a house or apartment from a normal agency or make direct contact with the sales department or sales personnel of the building.

41

您买几居的？
Nín mǎi jǐ jū de?
How many rooms would you like?

对话 Dialogue

A: 您买几居的？
Nín mǎi jǐ jū de?　How many rooms would you like?

B: 两居的。
Liǎng jū de.　I'd like two rooms.

类似说法 Similar Expressions

您买几室一厅？/您打算买多大面积的房？
How many rooms would you like to buy? / How many
square meters are you going to buy?

幽默 Humor

越大越好。　The bigger the better.

联想 Association

别墅/复式结构房/带花园的一层/四合院
villa/compound-system apartment/first floor with a gar-
den/Siheyuan courtyard house

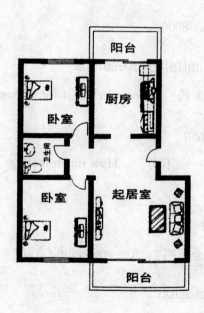

42

多少钱1平米?
Duōshǎo qián yì píngmǐ?
What is the price for one square meter?

对话 Dialogue

A: 多少钱1平米?
Duōshǎo qián yì píngmǐ?　What is the price for one square meter?

B: 8000。
Bāqiān.　8000.

类似说法 Similar Expressions

每平米多少钱?　How much is it for one square meter?

反义 Antonym

多少钱?——不卖。　How much is it? ——It is not for sale.

幽默 Humor

您这是卖金子吗?　Are you selling gold?

联想 Association

多少钱1个月? /多少钱1度电? /多少钱1吨水?
How much is it per month? / What is the price for electricity? / What is the price for water?

现在有的房子卖的是建筑面积，有的房子卖的是使用面积，在买房的时候您都必须综合考虑进去。此外，还得考虑地段、交通、生活设施等多方面因素。

Some houses are sold according to the floor space and others according to the internal area. All of these factors should be taken into consideration. Besides the size, location, the availability of transportation and the living environment should also be taken into account.

43

二手房便宜点儿。
Èr shǒu fáng piányi diǎnr.
Second-hand houses are cheaper.

对话 Dialogue

A:有便宜的吗？
   Yǒu piányi de ma?   Do you have anything cheaper?
B:二手房便宜点儿。
   Èr shǒu fáng piányi diǎnr.   Second-hand houses are
   cheaper.

类似说法 Similar Expressions

旧房便宜。 Old houses are cheaper.

反义 Antonym

便宜——贵 cheap——expensive

幽默 Humor

二环以内一张床，抵得上郊区一栋房。
A bed inside the 2nd Ring road is equal to a house in the
suburb.

联想 Association

平房/地下室/郊区/五环以外/烂尾楼/尾房
ranch house/ basement/ suburb/ outside the Fifth Ring/
unfinished building/ storage house

有的房子属于劣质工程,不能贪便宜而选择烂尾楼。二手房的价钱和新房相差不是很大,而且办手续烦琐,还有可能上当受骗,所以还不如挑选经济实用的新房。

Some houses are built of poor quality materials and can be purchased cheap. You are advised not to count on building quality. Second – hand houses are sold at a slightly cheaper price than new ones, but there is a lot of paperwork and it is easy to be cheated. It is better to choose newly-built houses.

44

可以看看房子吗?
Kěyǐ kànkan fángzi ma?
May I see the house?

对话 Dialogue

A：可以看看房子吗?
　　Kěyǐ kànkan fángzi ma?　May I see the house?
B：可以。
　　Kěyǐ.　Yes, of course.

类似说法 Similar Expressions

我想先看看房子。　I'd like to have a look at the house first.

反义 Antonym

可以——不行　Yes, of course——No, you can't.

幽默 Humor

一手交钱,一手交货。　Give me the cash, I will give you the goods.

联想 Association

房子/住宅/别墅　house/residence/villa

贴心提示 Tips

买房要先看房子，看房子要带着问题去，尤其是二手房，很多的细节都必须仔细地查看清楚。

Before you purchase a house or apartment, you should see the house first. Every detail should be examined carefully especially second-hand houses.

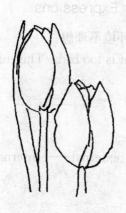

45

环境不好。
Huánjìng bù hǎo.
The environment is not good.

对话 Dialogue

A: 怎么样？
Zěnmeyàng?　What do you think of it?

B: 环境不好。
Huánjìng bù hǎo.　The environment is not good.

类似说法 Similar Expressions

环境太糟糕。/环境不理想。

The environment is too bad. /The enironment is not to my
expectation.

反义 Antonym

环境——内心　external——internal

幽默 Humor

我们这儿成垃圾站了。　We are like the garbage box.

联想 Association

闹市口/下风口　downtown area/leeward

住房周围的环境很重要,因为您每天的生活起居都在其中,所以选住房一定要考虑周围环境。

The surrounding environment of a house is of great importance since you will be living in it every day. It should be taken very seriously.

46

怎么样？
Zěnmeyàng?
What do you think of it?

对话 Dialogue

A:怎么样？
　Zěnmeyàng?　What do you think of it?
B:还行。
　Hái xíng.　It is okay.

类似说法 Similar Expressions

还 满 意 吗？/还 可 以 吧？/还 不 错 吧？　Are you satisfied? /Is that okay? /How is it?

反义 Antonym

怎么样？——不怎么样。　What do you think of it? —— I don't think it's very good.

幽默 Humor

除下水道不漏哪儿都漏。　Every pipe is leaking except the sewer.

联想 Association

劣质装修/精装修/毛坯房　bad fitment/ fit up finely/ unfinished house

看房子主要看朝向、结构，看门窗是否完好，房顶、墙壁有没有裂缝，水管、煤气管道是不是漏水、漏气，下水管道是不是通畅。

Seeing a house is mainly to see its direction and structure, to see whether the windows and doors are completely finished, whether there are slight cracks on the roof and walls, whether the water or gas pipes leak, and whether the sewer has a problem.

交 通
jiāo tōng **Transportation**

47

地铁在哪儿?
Dì tiě zài nǎr?
Where is the subway?

对话 Dialogue

A:地铁在哪儿?
　Dì tiě zài nǎr?　Where is the subway?

B:在左边。
　Zài zuǒ biān.　On your left.

类似说法 Similar Expressions

坐地铁怎么走?　How can I get to the subway station?

反义 Antonym

左边——右边　left——right

幽默 Humor

地铁在地底下。　Underground is surely under the ground.

联想 Association

地铁 1 号线/地铁 2 号线/直线地铁/环线地铁
subway line No. 1/line No. 2/straight line subway/
ring subway

在北京或其他大城市,乘坐地铁出行是最明智的选择,既快捷方便又经济实惠。初来乍到的人可以买一张或者自己画一张地铁线路图,特别要注意换乘车站的位置以便于顺利转车到达目的地。

In Beijing or other big cities, taking the subway is the most sensible choice as it is quick and economical. Newcomers can buy a map of the subway or draw one themselves. Please pay great attention to the change station so you may arrive at your destination quickly.

48 买 3 张。
Mǎi sān zhāng.
Three tickets please.

对话 Dialogue

A：买 3 张。

Mǎi sān zhāng.　Three tickets please.

B：您拿好。

Nín ná hǎo.　Here you are.

类似说法 Similar Expressions

要 3 张。/3 张。　I'd like three tickets. /Three please.

反义 Antonym

买——卖　buy——sell

幽默 Humor

我要坐两圈。　I will ride the route twice.

联想 Association

1 张/2 张/5 张　one/two/five tickets

北京地铁正在建设中,目前的票价比较复杂:1 号或 2 号线,包括在 1、2 号线之间换乘,票价是 3 元。只乘坐 13 号线车票也是 3 元。1、2 号线换乘八通线,票价 4 元。1、2 号线换乘 13 号线,票价 5 元。

坐地铁的人一般比较多,出门前别忘了准备一些零钱,以免因为找钱花去太多时间,也会耽误后面乘客的时间,更何况匆忙之间还担心找错钱。

Prices for subway ticket are a bit complicated as new lines in Beijing are constantly under construction. The prices for Line 1 and Line 2 including changes between them are 3 yuan. The price for Line 13 is also 3 yuan. If you are going to change from Line 1 or Line 2 to Line Batong, the total price will be 4 yuan. To change from Line 1 or Line 2 to Line 13, the total price will be 5 yuan.

It is usually very crowded in the subway. Please remember to bring change to pay your fare and avoid wasting your and other passengers' time. It is also easy to be given the wrong change when people are in a hurry.

49

北京站到了。
Běijīng zhàn dào le.
The next stop is Beijing Railway Station.

对话 Dialogue

A:北京站到了。
Běijīng zhàn dào le.　The next stop is Beijing Railway Station.

B:我们到了,走。
Wǒmen dào le, zǒu.　Here it is.

类似说法 Similar Expressions

咱到站了。/我们该下了。/到了快下车。
Here we are. /Time to get off. /Be quick to get out.

幽默 Humor

再坐一圈。Ride it for another round.

联想 Association

西直门站到了。/东直门站到了。/换乘车站到了。
The next stop is Xizhimen Station/Dongzhimen Station/change station.

98

地铁里有中、英文广播报站,如果您不太熟悉路,千万要注意听。地铁上下车的人比较多,站上停留时间比较短,下车前请做好准备。

The subway will announce the next stop in Chinese and English. If you are not familiar with the stops, please listen carefully. You'd better get ready in advance before getting off as it is crowded and the train only stops for very short time.

50 走哪边?
Zǒu nǎbiān?
Which direction to go?

对话 Dialogue

A: 走哪边?
Zǒu nǎbiān?　Which direction to go?

B: 走右边。
Zǒu yòu biān.　To your right.

类似说法 Similar Expressions

从哪儿出去? /往哪儿走?　Where is the way out? /
Which direction shall we go?

反义 Antonym

右边——左边　right——left

幽默 Humor

我晕头转向了。　I am confused and disoriented.

联想 Association

东北口/西北口/东南口/西南口/A、B、C、D 出口
north east exit/north west exit/south east exit/exit A、B、
C、D

　　北京的地铁站台上都有示意图,到达不同的地方应从不同的出口出去,这样可以节省很多时间。因此看地铁示意图非常重要。

　　There are signs on every subway platform which direct the way to the different exits. It may help save time to have a look at them before you exit.

还是地铁快。
Háishì dì tiě kuài.
Taking the subway is faster.

对话 Dialogue

A:还是地铁快。

Háishì dì tiě kuài. Taking the subway is faster.

B:就是。

Jiùshì. You are right.

类似说法 Similar Expressions

坐地铁比打的还快。 The subway is much faster than a taxi.

反义 Antonym

快——慢 fast——slow

幽默 Humor

惟一不堵的车真好。 It is great to take the only kind of transportation without traffic jams.

联想 Association

城铁/公交车/三轮车/出租车
city subway/bus/tricycle/taxi

在大城市,建议出行能坐地铁的尽量坐地铁,乘坐地铁不会遇到交通堵塞,节约的时间可以安排做别的事情。地铁不能直接到达的地方可以先乘地铁到离目的地最近的地方,然后再转乘公交车或者打的,如果不太远还可以步行。

In big cities it is recommended that you travel by the subway as much as possible because you can avoid traffic jams and save time. If there is no subway station at your destination, you may first take the subway to the nearest station and then change to a bus or taxi or even walk if it is not far.

52

打的去。
Dǎdī qù.
Let's take a taxi.

对话 Dialogue

A：要晚了！
Yào wǎn le!　We are going to be late!
B：打的去。
Dǎdī qù.　Let's take a taxi.

类似说法 Similar Expressions

坐出租车去。　go by taxi

反义 Antonym

打的——自己开车。　to take taxi——to drive by oneself

幽默 Humor

你买单就打。　We will take taxi if you pay.

联想 Association

坐地铁/坐公共汽车　to take subway/to take a bus

贴心提示 Tips

　　打的一般是为赶时间，或者没有直达的公共汽车，需要换好几次车。因为马路上经常塞车，打的也不一定就快，有地铁的地方还不如选择坐地铁。

Take a taxi when you are in a hurry or there is no direct bus. However, traffice jams often slow traffic so it is not always faster to take a taxi. If there is subway, you should take it.

53 您去哪儿?
Nín qù nǎr?
Where are you going?

对话 Dialogue

A:您去哪儿?
　　Nín qù nǎr?　Where are you going?
B:去北京大学。
　　Qù Běijīng Dàxué.　To Peking University.

类似说法 Similar Expressions

到哪儿去啊?／上哪儿?　Where to go?／Where to?

反义 Antonym

去——来　go——come

联想 Association

去西单。／去清华大学。／去东来顺吃涮羊肉。
to Xidan/to Chinghua University/to have Mongolian hot pot in Donglaishun Restaurant

目前北京的出租车价位有:1.20 元/公里、1.60 元/公里、2.00 元/公里三种,贴在车窗上的显著位置。您可以根据您的经济情况选择。

There are three types of taxis: 1.20 yuan per kilometer, 1.60 yuan per kilometer and 2.00 yuan per kilometer. You will see the price on the rear windows and can make your own choices.

54 北京大学哪个门？
Běijīng Dàxué nǎ ge mén?
Which gate of the Peking University?

对话 Dialogue

A: 北京大学哪个门？
Běijīng Dàxué nǎ ge mén? Which gate of the Peking University?

B: 东门。
Dōng mén. East gate.

类似说法 Similar Expressions

去北大哪个门？ Which gate are you going to at Peking University?

反义 Antonym

东门——西门 east gate——west gate

幽默 Humor

人最多的那个门。 The most crowded gate.

联想 Association

北大医学部/万柳校区/北大校园/未名湖/博雅塔/沙滩红楼 Department of Medical Science of Peking University/ 10-thousand-willow campus area/campus of Peking University/Wei Ming Lake/ Bo Ya Pagoda/ Sand Red Building

贴心提示 Tips

　　北京的许多大学都很大,进出有很多门,有的门不让进车。去之前最好问清楚从哪个门进去离目的地最近,否则会走很多的冤枉路。

There are many big universities in Beijing, each with several entrances. Some of the entrances are not for any vehicles. You'd better make it clear beforehand which gate is the nearest to your destination to avoid a long walk.

55 怎么走?
Zěnme zǒu?
How do I get there?

对话 Dialogue

A: 怎么走?
Zěnme zǒu?　How do I get there?
B: 随便您 。
Suíbiàn nín.　Suit yourself.

类似说法 Similar Expressions

从哪儿走? Which way to go?

反义 Antonym

走——停　go——stop

幽默 Humor

向前走。　Go straight ahead.

联想 Association

走/跑/飞　walk/run/fly

110

贴心提示 Tips

条条大路通罗马,到达目的地可能有多条路线。如果您对道路非常熟悉,可以提出意见;如果您不熟悉,可说"随便您"。

As the old saying notes, all roads lead to Rome. There are usually several routes to a destination. If you are very familiar with all the routes, you may give a suggestion. If you are not, simply say "suit yourself".

56 北大东门到了。
Běi Dà dōng mén dào le.
Here we come to the east gate of Beida.

对话 Dialogue

A：北大东门到了。
Běi Dà dōng mén dào le.　Here we come the east gate
of Beida（abbreviation of Peking University）.

B：好的。
Hǎo de.　Okay.

类似说法 Similar Expressions

到了，请下车吧。　We are here，please exit.

反义 Antonym

到了——没到　Here we are——We have not got to it.

联想 Association

到家了。/到站了。/到地方了。
We are home. / Here we are at your stop. / Here is the
place.

"北京大学"可以简称为"北大"。到目的地的时候,先看一下是不是您要去的地方,有时司机带错了路,还得再走好远的路呢。

Peking University can be abbreviated as "Beida". When you arrive, first check if you are at the right entrance or gate. Sometimes the driver may bring you to a different gate and the walk between gates can be a long one.

57

多少钱?
Duōshǎo qián?
How much?

对话 Dialogue

A: 多少钱?
　Duōshǎo qián?　How much?
B: 28 块。
　Èrshíbā kuài.　28 yuan.

反义 Antonym

多——少　much——little

幽默 Humor

我今天做义工。　I am a volunteer today.

联想 Association

人民币/美元/欧元　Renminbi/US dollar/Euro

　　"多少钱"是出门在外进行买卖活动时用得最多的一句话,您可一定要学好它,说准确。

　　"How much" is the most commonly used phrase when you are shopping. Learn to say it accurately please.

58

给您票。
Gěi nín piào.
Here is your ticket.

对话 Dialogue

A：给您钱。
　　Gěi nín qián.　Here is my payment.
B：给您票。
　　Gěi nín piào.　Here is your ticket.

类似说法 Similar Expressions

您拿好发票。　Hold your invoice carefully.

反义 Antonym

给您票。——不要票。　Here is your ticket.——I don't want it.

幽默 Humor

您给的是六合彩票吗？　Is it a lottery ticket?

联想 Association

发票/车票/门票　invoice/ ticket/ entrance ticket

交完打的车费后您千万保存好发票,如果下车之后才发现有东西落在车上,还可以按照发票上的车号去找。当然,最好是下车时把东西带全,省得以后着急。

Please remember to keep the taxi invoice because you may need to contact the taxi driver if you find you forgot to take some of your belongings with you when you exited. Of course the best thing is to remember to take all your belongings with you.

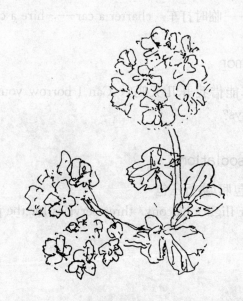

59

可以包车吗?
Kěyǐ bāo chē ma?
May I charter your car?

对话 Dialogue

A: 可以包车吗?
　　Kěyǐ bāo chē ma?　May I charter your car?
B: 可以 。
　　Kěyǐ.　Sure.

反义 Antonym

包车——临时打车　charter a car——hire a car

幽默 Humor

您这车能借我开几天吗?　Can I borrow your car for a
few days?

联想 Association

包机/包厢/实行三包
charter flight/ balcony/ three services for the price.

如果您想在北京多玩儿几天,又遇到了比较投缘的司机(我们习惯叫的哥、的姐),包几天车是个不错的主意。不仅仅是省钱;的哥还可以给您当导游,让您玩儿得痛快。有的外国朋友回国后还把自己认识的的哥介绍给亲朋好友;或者下次再来中国时仍然找他。

If you would like to stay several days longer in Beijing and are familiar with one taxi driver (customarily referred to as "Dige" for male drivers and "Dijie" for female drivers), reserving or chartering their car is a good idea. You may save money while the driver may act as a guide to give you a happy time. Some foreigners even pass on the name of the driver to their friends and relatives so they can hire them when they come to Beijing.

60

一天 200。
Yì tiān èrbǎi.
200 yuan a day.

对话 Dialogue

A：包车多少钱?
Bāo chē duōshǎo qián? How much does it cost to charter a car and driver?

B：一天 200。
Yì tiān èrbǎi. 200 yuan a day.

类似说法 Similar Expressions

200 块一天。/每天 200 块。 200 yuan a day. /200 yuan per day.

幽默 Humor

包月不包天。 Monthly rent is not counted by day.

联想 Association

150/300/400

包车一般都按天计算，天数多就会便宜些。包车的价格是时价，会因为各种因素而变动。

Hiring a car and driver, or chartering a car, usually means paying for each day you use the service. Chartering a car for a longer period will probably result in a cheaper rate. The price is flexible and will go up and down due to a number of factors.

61

明天行吗?

Míngtiān xíng ma?

Can we start tomorrow?

对话 Dialogue

A:明天行吗?

Míngtiān xíng ma? Can we start tomorrow?

B:行。

Xíng. Sure.

类似说法 Similar Expressions

明天就开始包车可以吗? Can I charter your car begin-

ning from tomorrow?

反义 Antonym

行——不行 sure——No,I am afraid I can't.

联想 Association

今天/昨天/后天 today/yesterday/the day after tomorrow

贴心提示 Tips

如果您相中了一位的哥，就马上定下来，并且和他商量好活动日程，这样您以后就省心多了。

If you like a taxi driver, you may negotiate a charter with him right away and tell him your schedule. This may save you a lot of time.

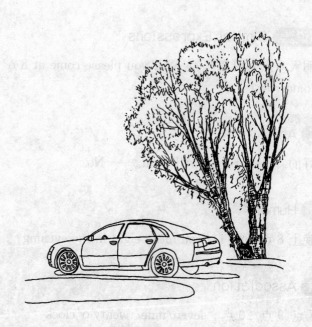

123

62

8 点来好吗?
Bā diǎn lái hǎo ma?
Would you please come at 8:00?

对话 Dialogue

A:8 点来好吗?
　Bā diǎn lái hǎo ma?　Would you please come at 8:00?
B:好的。
　Hǎo de.　All right.

类似说法 Similar Expressions

明天 8 点来可以吗?　Will you please come at 8 o'clock
tomorrow?

反义 Antonym

好的。——不行。　All right.——No.

幽默 Humor

晚上 8 点吗?　Do you mean eight in the evening?

联想 Association

7 点/9 点/20 点　seven/nine/twenty o'clock

124

定好了包车,再定好第二天出发的时间。别忘了交换电话号码,有什么事情好联系。

To charter a car, it is important to fix the time you require the car the next day. Don't forget to exchange telephone numbers so that you may contact each other in case of other unexpected changes.

63

明天见!
Míngtiān jiàn!
See you tomorrow!

对话 Dialogue

A:明天见!
　Míngtiān jiàn!　See you tomorrow!
B:明天见!
　Míngtiān jiàn!　See you tomorrow!

类似说法 Similar Expressions

明天再见!　See you tomorrow

反义 Antonym

见——不见　see——don't see

幽默 Humor

不见不散!　Be there or be square!

联想 Association

谢谢。/您慢走。　Thank you. /Mind your step.

126

贴心提示 Tips

　　这里的"明天见"是真的明天见面。有时候这么说和"再见"差不多,是礼貌用语。

　　"See you tomorrow" here in China really means people will meet each other tomorrow. Sometimes "see you tomorrow" is a polite salutation, just like "goodbye".

64 坐公交车。
Zuò gōng jiāo chē.
By bus.

see you tomorrow" then in China really means people will meet each other tomorrow. Sometimes "see you tomorrow" is a polite salut... goodbye.

对话 Dialogue

A: 咱们怎么去?
Zánmen zěnme qù? How do we get there?

B: 坐公交车。
Zuò gōng jiāo chē. By bus.

类似说法 Similar Expressions

坐公共汽车。/坐大公共。 To take bus/to take public bus.

反义 Antonym

坐车——走路 take a bus——on foot

幽默 Humor

坐 11 路。(两条腿走着去) Take Number 11. (to walk on foot)

联想 Association

坐地铁/打车 by subway/take a taxi

128

近道可以乘公交车,远道尽量利用地铁。北京的公交车非常多,但乘客也多;您如果怕挤,可以坐 8 字头的,因为带空调,票价贵一些,人也少。比如 800 内环、三环上的 830、可以到颐和园和北京大学的 801、到天安门和北京站的 802 等。

You may take a bus when your destination is close or ride the subway when it is far. There are various buses in Beijng and they are often packed. If you prefer less crowded transportation, you may pay more and choose a bus numbered 8XX as it will be less crowded and have air conditioning. Buses like this are, for example, No. 800 on the Internal Ring, No. 830 on the Third Ring, No. 801 to the Summer Palace and Peking University, No. 802 to Tian'anmen and Beijng Railway Station and etc.

对话 Dialogue

A：您到哪儿？

　　Nín dào nǎr?　Where to go?

B：北京站。

　　Běijīng Zhàn.　to the Beijing Railway Station.

类似说法 Similar Expressions

您去哪儿？/您哪儿下？/您上哪儿？

Where are you going? /Where are you getting off? /
Where is your destination?

幽默 Humor

车不走了我就到了。I shall arrive when the bus does.

联想 Association

北京西站/北京南站/北京北站/北京东站

Beijing West/South/North/East Railway Station

130

在乘公交车之前,先看清楚站牌上的站名,还不清楚再问售票员。有时同一个站名,可能分布在不同的方向。所以要把你要到达的确切地址告诉售票员,以免走错了。

Before getting on a bus, please check the name of the stop or even ask the conductor. Sometimes different places may have the same name. You need to ask the conductor how to get to your destination.

66 两块一位。
Liǎng kuài yí wèi.
2 yuan for one person

of the stop or even ask the conductor
different places may have the same name. You need
to act the conductor how to get to your destination.

对话 Dialogue

A:两块一位。
Liǎng kuài yí wèi. 2 yuan for one person.
B:要两张。
Yào liǎng zhāng. Two tickets please.

类似说法 Similar Expressions

一张两块。 2 yuan for one ticket.

幽默 Humor

真便宜! It is next to nothing!

联想 Association

空调车/2元起价的车/1元起价的车/中巴
air-conditioned bus/ 2-yuan minimum bus/ 1-yuan minimum bus/ minibus

贴心提示 Tips

公交车票一般都比较便宜,市内1路－124路一律1元;8字头带空调的2元起价……上车前最好准备零钱,尤其是无人售票车,没有零钱就上不去了。在北京乘坐公交车买完票后还要收好,以备下车查票。

Bus tickets are often comparatively cheap. They are priced at 1 yuan only for Line No.1 to No. 124 and 2 yuan starting for all lines of 8XX. You'd better have a supply of small change as some buses require you to put the fare into a box. If you buy a ticket on the bus, please keep the receipt when getting off.

67

到了请叫我们。
Dào le qǐng jiào wǒmen.
Please let us know when we arrive.

对话 Dialogue

A：到了请叫我们。

Dào le qǐng jiào wǒmen. Please let us know when we arrive.

B：好的。

Hǎo de. All right.

类似说法 Similar Expressions

到站了告诉我们一下。 Please tell us when the time comes.

幽默 Humor

到终点站不用叫。 It is not necessary to call us if it is the final stop.

联想 Association

叫/喊/嚷 call/shout/cry

如果您不熟悉那条路线,您一定要注意听报站名,或者请求售票员到站时叫您,以免坐过站。

If you do not know how to identify your destination, please listen to the announcement or ask the conductor to tell you when to get off.

68

北京站到了，两位请下车。

Běijīng Zhàn dào le, liǎng wèi qǐng xià chē.

The next stop is Beijing Railway Station.

You two may get off.

对话 Dialogue

A:北京站到了，两位请下车。

　Běijīng Zhàn dào le, liǎng wèi qǐng xià chē.

　The next stop is Beijing Railway Station. You two may get off.

B:谢谢。

　Xièxiè. Thank you.

类似说法 Similar Expressions

两位朋友到站了。 Time for two friends to get off.

反义 Antonym

下车——上车 get off——get on

幽默 Humor

你的家到了。 This stop will be your home.

联想 Association

西直门/保利剧院/国家大剧院/工人体育馆/亚运村
Xizhimen/ Poly Theatre/National Grand Theatre/
Worker's Stadium/Asian Games Village

贴心提示 Tips

乘公交车的时候注意坐稳或站稳扶好,注意保管好随身携带的财物,不要给小偷可乘之机。

When you take the bus, please stand steadily and maintain your balance by holding on to the supporting rail or handhold. Keep your belongings in sight to avoid having them stolen.

69 坐人力车。
Zuò rénlì chē.
Take a rickshaw

对话 Dialogue

A: 怎么去？
　 Zěnme qù?　How to get there?
B: 坐人力车。
　 Zuò rénlì chē.　Take a rickshaw.

类似说法 Similar Expressions

去那儿没公交车怎么办？　How can we go if there is no bus?

反义 Antonym

人力车——电动车　rickshaw——electromotive vehicle

幽默 Humor

跑吧！　Let's run!

联想 Association

三轮车/脚踏车/骆驼祥子　tricycle/bicycle/Camel Xiangzi

短距离坐公交车不方便可以选择坐人力车,人力车坐着舒服、敞亮,观景清楚,但是要提醒蹬车师傅注意安全,不要违章行驶。

A rickshaw can be taken for short trip. It is comfortable and provides a clear view of the scenery. You may remind the driver to drive safely and observe traffic regulations.

70 后海多少钱?
Hòuhǎi duōshǎo qián?
How much is it for Houhai?

对话 Dialogue

A: 后海多少钱?
Hòuhǎi duōshǎo qián?　How much is it for Houhai?
B: 5块。
Wǔ kuài.　5 yuan.

类似说法 Similar Expressions

后海几块?　How much for Houhai?

幽默 Humor

后海可贵了。　It is very expensive for Houhai.

联想 Association

北海/西海/什刹海　Beihai/Xihai/Shishahai

　　坐三轮车一般都比较便宜，在打的和公交车之间，如果距离比较短，打车不合算，就可以找三轮车，但三轮车不是哪儿都有，地铁附近一般有，主干道上不让停三轮车。后海一带的胡同游三轮车最有名，也最漂亮、最讲究。

The price for a rickshaw is often between that of taxi fare and a bus ticket. If destination is not too far and it is not worth taking a taxi, you may take a rickshaw. Rickshaws often stay at subway stations. Rickshaws for a Hutong Tour around Houhai District are the most famous and beautifully-decorated.

坐好了吗?
Zuò hǎo le ma?
Are you ready?

对话 Dialogue

A:坐好了吗?
　Zuò hǎo le ma?　Are you ready?
B:坐好了,可以走了。
　Zuò hǎo le,kěyǐ zǒu le.　Ready,let's go.

类似说法 Similar Expressions

坐稳了吗?　Are you ready?

反义 Antonym

好——没好　okay——wait a minute

幽默 Humor

那我就撒丫子了啊。　Then I shall run to my extreme.

联想 Association

同学们坐好准备上课了。/准备开会了。/都到齐了吗?
The students are ready to have a class. /Now let's have a
meeting. /Is everybody here?

142

贴心提示 Tips

叮嘱三轮车师傅千万骑慢点儿，注意交通安全。

Please warn the driver of the rickshaw to keep a slow speed and be careful of the traffic.

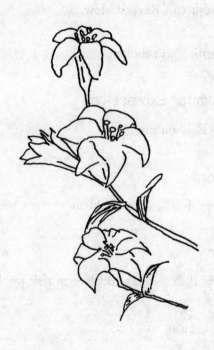

72

没问题。

Méi wèntí.

No problem.

对话 Dialogue

A:慢点儿骑。

Màn diǎnr qí. Keep it slow.

B:没问题。

Méi wèntí. No problem.

类似说法 Similar Expressions

放心吧。 Rely on me.

反义 Antonym

没问题——不保险 no problem——not reliable

幽默 Humor

我可不敢玩儿命。 I do not dare to risk my life.

联想 Association

过马路/挤公交/雨天开车/雪后驾车

get through the road/take a bus/drive on rainy days/drive
after a snow

144

"没问题"曾经是 2002 年带领中国足球队出线的米卢教练会说的几句汉语之一,他确实做到了,中国球迷永远感谢他。希望您也能学会,并且能够兑现。但是,这话也可能有水分,不能全信;听其言,还要观其行。

"No problem" was one of several sentences the former Chinese Football Coach Milunosevich learned to say. He took the Chinese Football Team to the 2002 World Cup. Chinese football fans will forever thank him for this. We also hope you will learn to say it and keep the phrase in mind. But we cannot trust what people say until we see their actions.

73

到了，您慢点儿下。
Dào le, nín màn diǎnr xià.
Here we are, be careful getting off.

对话 Dialogue

A: 到了，您慢点儿下。
Dào le, nín màn diǎnr xià. Here we are, be careful getting off.

B: 给您 5 块。
Gěi nín wǔ kuài. Here is 5 yuan.

类似说法 Similar Expressions

您慢走。 Mind your step.

反义 Antonym

慢——快 slow——quick

幽默 Humor

再拉一圈吧。 Another round please.

联想 Association

10 块/15 块/20 块 ten/fifteen/twenty yuan

人力车夫很辛苦,凭体力赚钱,当您恻隐之心发起时,可以适当给点小费。

Rickshaw boys live a hard life. If you have pity on them, you may tip them.

74

请拿好东西。

Qǐng ná hǎo dōngxi.

Please take your belongings.

对话 Dialogue

A：请拿好东西。

　　Qǐng ná hǎo dōngxi.　Please take your belongings.

B：谢谢。

　　Xièxie.　Thank you.

类似说法 Similar Expressions

别忘了您的东西。　Don't forget your belongings.

幽默 Humor

这些东西是送给我的吗？　Are these gifts for me?

联想 Association

寻物启事/失物招领/拾金不昧

notice for a missing person/lost-and-found notice/return money found

中国一向以文明礼仪之邦著称,对待别人的热情和礼貌要有相应的表示,一般说声"谢谢"。

China has a long history of civilized behavior and polite manners. We always show our gratitude in response to another's best wishes and help and we are likely to say: "Thank you".

寻物启事

75 太远了。
Tài yuǎn le.
It is too far.

对话 Dialogue

A：走着去？
Zǒu zhe qù?   Let's go there on foot.
B：太远了。
Tài yuǎn le. It is too far.

类似说法 Similar Expressions

有点儿远。/那可远了。 It's a bit far. / That's very far from here.

反义 Antonym

远——近 far——close

幽默 Humor

那明天也到不了。 I can't reach there even tomorrow.

联想 Association

散步/小跑/马拉松 walk/jog/marathon

在大城市,出门去某个地方,有时感觉上认为是一小段路,实际上要走很长的时间。一般认为,半小时还不能走到的就算远,需要借助交通工具。当然愿意走路锻炼身体那就是另外一回事了。

In big cities, it always takes a long time to get somewhere. Sometimes you think it is not far away, but actually it will take a long walk to get there. We generally consider it far when it takes more than half an hour's walk, and if it is more than that we use another mode of transportation. Of course this general rule does not apply when you walk to exercise.

76 太近。
Tài jìn.
It is too close.

对话 Dialogue

A：打的去?
Dǎdí qù?　Let's go by taxi.

B：太近。
Tài jìn.　It is too close.

类似说法 Similar Expressions

不算远。　not far

反义 Antonym

近——远　close——far

幽默 Humor

刚在车里坐稳就到了。　I just sit here and we arrive.

联想 Association

骑车/滑板　ride a bicycle/skateboard

一般认为,5 公里以内的路程就算近,打的不合算。

It is generally considered close when your destination is within 5 kilometers, in which case it is not worth taking a taxi.

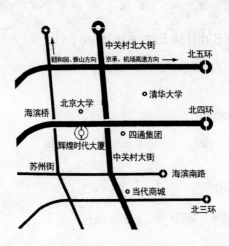

77 骑自行车去?
Qí zìxíngchē qù?
Let's get there by bicycle.

对话 Dialogue

A:骑自行车去?

　Qí zìxíngchē qù?　Let's get there by bicycle.

B:好。

　Hǎo.　Okay.

类似说法 Similar Expressions

开车去/打车去　drive/take a taxi

反义 Antonym

骑车——步行　ride a bike——walk

幽默 Humor

你带着我？　Will you carry me?

联想 Association

28 载重自行车/跑车/变速车/折叠自行车/斜杠自行车
bicycle to haul goods - size 28/sports bicycle/speed-shift
bicycle/folded bicycle/lightweight bicycle

坐公交车不便,走着去太远、打的去又太近的地方,一般可以骑自行车去。中国号称自行车王国,您来到中国也不妨骑骑自行车,体验一下骑车族的生活。

If there is no bus, and the distance is too far to walk and too close to take a taxi, you may ride a bicycle. China is known as the Kingdom of Bicycles. You should try to ride a bicycle while you are here just for the experience.

78

买车还是租车?
Mǎi chē hái shì zū chē?
Would you like to buy or rent a car?

对话 Dialogue

A:买车还是租车?
Mǎi chē hái shì zū chē?　Would you like to buy or rent a car?

B:租车。
Zū chē. Rent.

类似说法 Similar Expressions

您需要什么样的服务?　What can I do to help you?

反义 Antonym

买——租　buy——rent

幽默 Humor

租车不如蹭车。　Hitchhiking is better than renting.

联想 Association

买车贷款/停车场/耗油量/高速公路
car loan/parking lot/consumption of gasoline/speedway

156

贴心提示 Tips

临时在大城市居住可以租车,长期居住的可以考虑买一辆车,但是大城市内的交通太拥堵了,买车或租车有的时候会带来一系列的烦恼。

You may rent a car for a temporary stay in big cities and buy a car if you are living here for a long period. Please note, however, that traffic in big cities makes driving and parking difficult and owning or renting a car may cause a lot of trouble.

79

租什么车？
Zū shénme chē?
What kind of car would you like to rent?

对话 Dialogue

A：租什么车？
　Zū shénme chē?　What kind of car would you like to rent?
B：小车。
　Xiǎo chē.　Car.

类似说法 Similar Expressions

租什么样的？　What kinds do you rent?

幽默 Humor

租法拉利怎么样？　How about renting a Fararri?

联想 Association

国产车/日产车/欧美车　domestic car/Japanese car/Euro-American car

贴心提示 Tips

　　租车也要量力而行，看用途。假如是郊游，国产车就行了；如果是去机场接朋友，可以考虑租辆好车，让朋友觉得你对他很尊重。

When you rent a car, you should first think about why you need the car. If you are only on a trip, a domestic car is good enough. If you are to pick up your friends at the airport, a more expensive car may be required to show your respect for them.

80

最贵的多少钱？
Zuì guì de duōshǎo qián?
What is the most expensive?

对话 Dialogue

A：最贵的多少钱？
Zuì guì de duōshǎo qián?　What is the most expensive?

B：一天 1000。
Yì tiān yìqiān.　1000 yuan per day.

类似说法 Similar Expressions

最好的车什么价？　What is the price of the best car?

反义 Antonym

贵——便宜　expensive——cheap

幽默 Humor

是带司机的吗？　Will a driver be included with the car?

联想 Association

800/900/2000

　　租车的价格是浮动的,您可以上网了解行情,还可以货比三家。

The rates for car rental vary. You may browse the net for information about this and make your own comparison of rates.

81

最便宜的多少钱?
Zuì piányi de duōshǎo qián?
What is the cheapest?

对话 Dialogue

A:最便宜的多少钱?
Zuì piányi de duōshǎo qián? What is the cheapest?

B:最便宜的140。
Zuì piányi de yìbǎi sì.

The cheapest costs 140 yuan.

类似说法 Similar Expressions

档次低点的是多少? How much is the price for an economy model car?

反义 Antonym

便宜——昂贵 cheap——expensive

幽默 Humor

能开上马路吗? Can it really go on the street?

联想 Association

奥拓/夏利/长安铃木 Alto/Xiali/Chang'an Mitsubishi

租车要确保车的质量，其实车的档次是其次，关键是车的性能要好，刹车、油门等都要确保安全。

When renting a car, the most important thing is to pay attention to its quality and function rather than its status. Be sure that it has good brakes and accelerator.

玩 乐
wán lè **Entertainment**

82

天气真好!
Tiānqì zhēn hǎo!
What a nice day!

对话 Dialogue

A: 天气真好!
  Tiānqì zhēn hǎo!   What a nice day!
B: 出去走走!
  Chūqù zǒuzǒu!   Let's go for a walk.

类似说法 Similar Expressions

大晴天!   What a sunny day!

反义 Antonym

真好——真坏   really good——really bad

幽默 Humor

不出去对不起上帝。   If we are not going out, we will offend God.

联想 Association

春光明媚/秋高气爽   splendid spring scenery/the autumn sky is clear and the air is bracing

多做户外活动,有利身体健康。只要天气允许,建议您尽量多出去走走。

Outdoor exercise is beneficial to your health. We suggest you go out as often as possilbe if the weather permits.

83

上公园。
Shàng gōngyuán.
To the park.

对话 Dialogue

A：上哪儿?
　Shàng nǎr?　Where shall we go?
B：上公园。
　Shàng gōngyuán.　To the park.

类似说法 Similar Expressions

去公园吧。　Let's go to the park.

反义 Antonym

上公园。——不上公园。　go to the park——do not go to
the park

幽默 Humor

上天吧。　Go to heaven.

联想 Association

颐和园/香山/北海/圆明园/天坛
the Summer Palace/Fragrant Hill/Beihai Park/the Old
Summer Palace/Temple of Heaven

去公园最好避开节假日,因为人太多,会影响您的游兴。除了有名的公园,比如:颐和园、北海、天坛……建议您也可以去一些票价便宜的公园。比如紫竹院,门票 2 元,有山有水,植被丰富;公园内有个园中园筠石苑,门票 1 元,苑中石重水复,竹暗花明,是闹市中取静的绝好去处。

We recommend that you do not go to parks during holidays because of the crowds. The more famous parks, such as the Summer Palace, Beihai Park, Temple of Heaven, may also be cheaper to visit during regular weekdays. Zizhuyuan Park (Purple Bamboo Park) is one of these, with an entrance ticket priced at 2 yuan, it has small hills, lakes and plenty of plants. Inside there is a small yard called Junshiyuan priced at 1 yuan, where you may see stones, a fountain, bamboo and flowers. It is a fairly quiet place.

要 3 张票。
Yào sān zhāng piào.
Three tickets please.

对话 Dialogue

A:要 3 张票。
　Yào sān zhāng piào.　Three tickets please.
B:给您。
　Gěi nín.　Here you are.

类似说法 Similar Expressions

买 3 张。/拿 3 张。/给我 3 张票。
buy 3 tickets/bring me 3 tickets /give me 3 tickets

反义 Antonym

要——不要　want——do not want

幽默 Humor

我是 VIP。　I am a VIP.

联想 Association

要吃/要喝/要休息　want to eat/drink/have a break
通票/年票/季票/月票/淡季/旺季
through ticket/annual ticket/quarterly ticket/monthly
ticket/slack season/midseason

168

有的公园卖通票,意思是一张票可以进园中园。比如动物园就可以进熊猫馆。天坛可以进祈年殿。有的公园门票分淡季、旺季:

淡季是 11 月—3 月,票价比较便宜。比如颐和园是 20 元、动物园是 10 元。

旺季是 4 月—10 月,票价比较贵。比如颐和园是 30 元、动物园是 15 元。

Some parks will offer inclusive tickets that allow you to visit the entire park, including separate scenic areas normally requiring an additional charge. For example in the Beijing Zoo an inclusive ticket will include permission to enter the Panda Hall, and in Temple of Heaven you may enter the Hall of Prayer for Good Harvest. Some parks set different ticket prices for different seasons:

During the slack tourist season——from November to March, the price is lower.

The Summer Palace: 20 yuan; Beijing Zoo: 10 yuan

In midseason - from April to October, the price is higher.

The Summer Palace: 30 yuan; Beijing Zoo: 15 yuan

85 上船吗?
Shàng chuán ma?
Will you take a boat?

对话 Dialogue

A: 上船吗?

Shàng chuán ma?　Will you take a boat?

B: 上。

Shàng.　Yes, I will.

类似说法 Similar Expressions

划船吗?　Do you want to go boating?

反义 Antonym

上——下　above——under

幽默 Humor

我是旱鸭子,可别掉水里。　I am a non-swimmer, don't drown me.

联想 Association

上汽车/上飞机　get on bus/board a plane

170

公园的游船分好多种。大船是游览观光性质,游客不用划船。小船大致分三种:手划的、脚踏的、电瓶船,您可以根据兴趣爱好选择。虽然公园里的水都比较浅,但是如果你不会游泳的话,还是要多加小心。

There are several types of boats available in the parks. The bigger boats are for sightseeing. Three kinds of small boats are provided for visitors to select from: a row boat, a pedal-powered boat and an electric-powered boat. The lakes in the park are not very deep, however, you must take extra care if you can not swim.

86

那花真好看!
Nà huā zhēn hǎo kàn!
The flower is so beautiful!

86

对话 Dialogue

A：那花真好看!
　Nà huā zhēn hǎo kàn!　The flower is so beautiful!
B：就是。
　Jiùshì.　You are absolutely right.

类似说法 Similar Expressions

真漂亮/真美/真艳丽　really good-looking/really gorgeous/really bright-colored

反义 Antonym

真好看——真难看　good-looking——ugly

联想 Association

郁金香/牡丹/樱花/梅花/兰花
tulip/peony/cherry blossom/plum blossom/orchid

花很多,有的很好看却没有什么香味儿,有的虽香却不大好看,有的香味儿很浓,有的是淡的,要在远处才闻得到。北京市的市花是菊花和月季。

There are many kinds of flowers. Some are beautiful but have no fragrance while others are fragrant but not beautiful. Some have an intense fragrance, some smell so lightly that you can only smell it from far away. The city flower of Beijing is the chrysanthemum and the Chinese rose.

87

今天去寺庙吗？
Jīntiān qù sìmiào ma?
Will you go to the temples today?

对话 Dialogue

A：今天去寺庙吗？
Jīntiān qù sìmiào ma?　Will you go to the temples today?

B：好的。
Hǎo de.　Yes, I will.

类似说法 Similar Expressions

去参观寺庙吗？　Are you going to visit temples?

反义 Antonym

去——不去　go——do not go

幽默 Humor

白天逛庙，晚上睡觉。　In the day we go around the temples and at night we sleep.

联想 Association

庙/观/寺/庵/院　joss house/Taoist temple/temple/nunnery/cloister

北京的寺庙很多,市内的主要有:

妙应寺,俗称白塔寺,位于阜城门内大街路北。妙应寺白塔是元大都保存至今的重要标志,是中国现存最早最大的一座藏式佛塔。

法源寺,在宣武区法源寺后街,宣武门外教子胡同南端的东侧,它是北京市内现存最古老、规模最大的、历史最悠久的名刹。

广济寺,位于西城区西四路口西北角,现为中国佛教协会所在地,是全国佛教事务活动的中心。

雍和宫,位于东城区安定门东大街和雍和宫大街交汇处,它是北京地区规模最大、保存最完好的喇嘛教黄教寺院。雍和宫内紫檀木雕刻的罗汉山;白檀木雕刻的弥勒大佛;金丝楠木雕刻的佛龛,被誉为雍和宫内的木雕"三绝"。如果您去参观,可要抓住机会,仔细欣赏哦!

北京孔庙,坐落在北京仅存的唯一一条仍保持着清代北京古老街巷风貌的国子监街上。在雍和宫的西边。

白云观,位于西城区白云路,是北京第一大道观。现为中国道教协会所在地。

东岳庙,位于朝阳门外大街路北,是中国北方最大的"正一派"道观。东岳庙有"京城小碑林"之称。

如果您赶上春节在北京,还可以逛逛庙会。白云观的庙会就很有名。

There are many temples in Beijing. The main urban temples are as follows:

Miaoying Temple, also known as White Dagoba, is located north of Fuchengmennei Dajie. The White

Dagoba at Miaoying Temple is an important historical symbol built during the Yuan Dynasty and it is the earliest and largest extant example of a Tibetan-style Buddhist stupa.

Fayuan Temple, located in Fayuansi Houjie of Xuanwu District, is to the east of the southern end of Jiaozi Hutong on Xuanwumenwai. It is the oldest and most celebrated large scale temple still standing in downtown Beijing.

Guangji Temple is situated to the northwest of the Xisi crossroads in the Xicheng District. It now houses the China Buddhist Association and is a center for holding national Buddhist ceremonies and activities.

Yonghe Lamasery is located at the crossroads of the Andingmen East Street and Yonghegong Street in Dongcheng District. It is the biggest and best-preserved temple of Yellow Hat Lamaism in Beijing. It has carvings referred to as the "three matchless treasures," which include a carving of the Five-Hundred-Arhat-Hill made of red sandalwood, a statue of the Maitreya Buddha carved from a single piece of white sandalwood and a niche for the buddha carved from a nanmu tree. If you plan to go, please remember to have a good look at these.

The Confucius Temple in Beijing is located on

Guozijian Street, which is the only street that still preserves the look of the old Beijing streets during the Qing Dynasty. It is to the west of the Yonghe Lamasery.

Baiyunguan Temple is situated on Baiyunlu Street in the Xicheng District and is the largest Daoist temple of Beijing. It now houses the China National Daoist Association.

Dongyue Temple, situated in the north side of Chaoyangmenwai Street, is the largest Daoist temple of Zhengyipai in the north of China. It is also called the 'Stonehenge' Forest of Beijing.

If you are in Beijing during the Spring Festival, you can visit the Temple Fairs——a traditional way to celebrate the lunar new year. The Temple Fair at Baiyunguan Temple is a notable one.

88

古树真好!
Gǔ shù zhēn hǎo!
The ancient tree is great!

对话 Dialogue

A: 古树真好!
   Gǔ shù zhēn hǎo!   The ancient tree is great!

B: 就是!
   Jiùshì! Exactly!

类似说法 Similar Expressions

这古树真不错! The ancient tree is pretty good!

反义 Antonym

古树——新树苗   ancient tree——sapling

幽默 Humor

对着树许个愿吧。 Make a vow to the tree.

联想 Association

古松/古柏/古庙/古建筑   ancient pinetree/cypress/
ancient temple/ancient architecture

中国有很多几百年、上千年的古树，它们都是真正的国宝，中国历史的见证物。寺庙内外多古树参天，四季常青。比如怀柔红螺寺的御竹林、雌雄银杏、紫藤寄松，门头沟潭柘寺的柘树、古柏、银杏等等都非常有名。另外天坛公园的古柏也非常多，您可千万要去古柏林中走走啊！

There are many ancient trees that have been growing for some hundreds and thousands of years in China. These trees are the treasures of the country and witnesses to Chinese history. They are often found both inside and outside of the temple yards. The most famous are Emperor Bamboo Forests, monoecism gingko, wisteria autoecious of pinetree in Hongluo Temple (Red Trumpet Temple) of Huairou county; mulberry trees, ancient cypress, ancient gingko in Tanzhe Temple of Mentougou District. In addition, the Temple of Heaven also has many ancient cypress trees. You'd better go to walk around these places.

89

我要烧香。
Wǒ yào shāoxiāng.
I want to burn joss sticks.

对话 Dialogue

A: 我要烧香。
Wǒ yào shāoxiāng.　I want to burn joss sticks.

B: 我也要。
Wǒ yě yào.　So do I.

类似说法 Similar Expressions

上香/焚香　to burn sticks/ to burn incense

反义 Antonym

烧香——禁香
to burn sticks——to prohibit burning sticks

幽默 Humor

我有心香一炷。　I burnt a stick in the heart.

联想 Association

拜佛/磕头　to make a courtesy call to Buddha/to kowtow

　　入乡随俗是一句有道理的话，如果你同意的话，就烧烧香、磕磕头、许许愿，老天一定会给你好运的！如果你如了愿，可千万别忘了还愿！

　　It makes sense to "do in Rome as the Romans do." If you agree to this saying, you may burn joss sticks, kowtow and make a vow to a god and it will bring you good luck! If your wishes are fulfilled, please remember to thank the god!

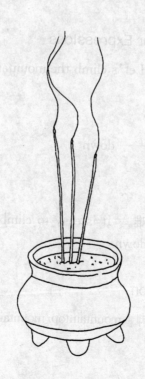

90 上山吗？
Shàng shān ma?
Do you want to climb the mountain?

It makes sense to do it alone as the Romans do." If you agree to this saying, you'd better just do it now by and make a vow to a good bring you good luck. If you please remember to thank the god!

对话 Dialogue

A：上山吗？

　　Shàng shān ma?　Do you want to climb the mountain?

B：上。

　　Shàng.　Yes, I do.

类似说法 Similar Expressions

上山好不好？　Let's climb the mountain, shall we?

反义 Antonym

上——下　up——down

幽默 Humor

上山容易下山难。　It is easy to climb the mountain and difficult to go down.

联想 Association

山顶/山腰/山脚　mountaintop/mountainside/foot of mountain

182

爬山前要做好准备工作,比如穿旧运动鞋、运动衣、棉袜子。少背行李,多带水。

Before climbing the mountain, please be well-prepared, wearing old sports shoes, sportswear and cotton stockings. Remember to bring a small pack and enough water.

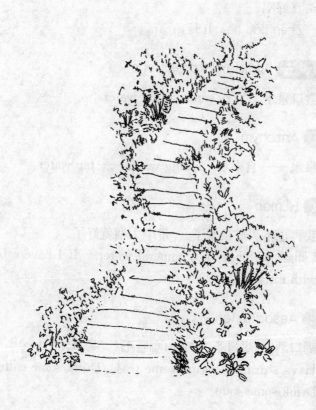

91 喝口山泉水。
Hē kǒu shānquán shuǐ.
Drink some spring water.

对话 Dialogue

A: 喝口山泉水。

Hē kǒu shānquán shuǐ.　Drink some spring water.

B: 真好喝。

Zhēn hǎo hē.　It is great.

类似说法 Similar Expressions

尝口泉水。　Try some spring water.

反义 Antonym

泉水——自来水　spring water——tap water

幽默 Humor

我再也不买矿泉水了。/带个大桶就好了。

I shall no longer buy mineral water. / If I have a barrel with me.

联想 Association

喝口酒。/喝口茶。/喝口咖啡吧！/喝口汤吧！

Have a drink! /Drink some tea! /Drink some coffee! / Drink some soup!

山间流出的泉水是很甜美的。现在,有好多城里人一大早就到山里去打泉水,您可以试试借用他们的打水工具。

Spring water in the mountains tastes very sweet. Now many city citizens go to fetch it in the early mornings. You may borrow a utensil or glass from them to have a taste of the water.

92

不好走。
Bù hǎo zǒu.
It is hard to walk.

对话 Dialogue

A：不好走。
Bù hǎo zǒu. It is hard to walk.

B：拉我一下。
Lā wǒ yí xià. Give me a helping hand.

类似说法 Similar Expressions

真难走。/爬不动了。 It is really difficult to walk. / I can not go on climbing.

反义 Antonym

走——停 go——stop

幽默 Humor

缺乏锻炼。 Not enough exercise.

联想 Association

跑/跳/蹦/跨 run/jump/leap/stride

贴心提示 Tips

不好走的路就要小心，不要逞能，安全第一！

Please be extremely careful on mountanous paths. Don't show off, remember safety first!

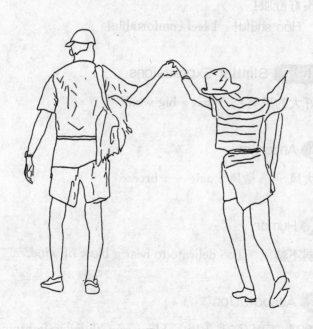

93

风好大！
Fēng hǎo dà!
It is windy!

对话 Dialogue

A:风好大！
　Fēng hǎo dà!　It is windy!
B:好舒服！
　Hǎo shūfu!　I feel comfortable!

类似说法 Similar Expressions

好大的风啊！　What a big wind!

反义 Antonym

大风——微风　gale——breeze

幽默 Humor

弱不禁风　Too delicate to bear a blow of wind.

联想 Association

刮风/下雨/打雷/闪电　blow/rain/thunder/lightning

北京一般不会有台风，只要不是沙尘暴，只管吹风，没什么大问题。

Beijing does not generally experience typhoons. As long as it does not create sand-dust storms, the wind will not cause any problems.

94

下雨了。
Xià yǔ le.
It's been raining.

A：下雨了。
Xià yǔ le. It's been raining.
B：买件雨衣。
Mǎi jiàn yǔyī. You need to buy a raincoat.

类似说法 Similar Expressions

来雨了！ It's going to rain.

反义 Antonym

下雨了。——雨停了。 It's been raining——It stopped raining.

幽默 Humor

这回把洗车的钱省了。 It saves money，I do not have to wash the car.

联想 Association

雨衣/雨伞/雨鞋 raincoat/umbrella/rain boot

现在旅游点都有卖雨具的。爬山时，如果下雨了，买件一次性雨衣最实用。

Rain gear is sold in every tourist spot. If it begins to rain when you are climbing the mountain, it is easy for you to buy a disposable raincoat.

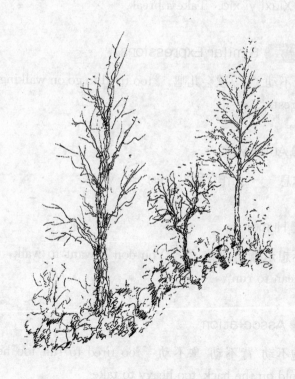

95

休息一下。
Xiūxi yí xià.
Take a break.

对话 Dialogue

A:不想走了。
Bù xiǎng zǒu le.　Don't want to go.

B:休息一下。
Xiūxi yí xià.　Take a break.

类似说法 Similar Expressions

走不动了。/歇会儿吧。　too tired to go on walking/Have a rest.

反义 Antonym

休息——工作/活动　rest——work

幽默 Humor

不想走就是想跑了?　You don't want to walk, do you mean to run?

联想 Association

跑不动/背不动/拿不动　too tired to run/too heavy to hold on the back/too heavy to take

咬牙坚持是一种锻炼，累了就歇会儿也是一种好办法，反正不必太勉强自己。

In case you feel tired doing exercises, you may choose either to go on exercising or to take a break. Remember, it is not necessary to force yourself.

96

真热!
Zhēn rè!
It is really hot!

对话 Dialogue

A:真热!
　Zhēn rè!　It is really hot!
B:小心感冒!
　Xiǎoxīn gǎnmào!　Be careful not to catch cold!

类似说法 Similar Expressions

热死了!　It's too hot.

反义 Antonym

热——冷　hot——cold

幽默 Humor

冬练三九,夏练三伏,要的就是这劲儿。
We aim to exercise in the coldest and hottest environments.

联想 Association

冷/凉/闷　cold/cool/humid

194

爬山的时候出些汗对身体有好处。但是山上风大，要在背风的地方休息；如果是冷天，要加件衣服，小心着凉感冒。

To work up a sweat while climbing a mountain is good for your health. Since there is usually a strong wind on the top of the mountain, please remember to take break on the side that is protected from the wind. You may need to put on one more layers of clothing to avoid catching a chill if it is cool.

97

真美!
Zhēn měi!
It is so pretty!

对话 Dialogue

A:真美!
Zhēn měi!　It is so pretty!
B:太美了!
Tài měi le!　It is gorgeous!

类似说法 Similar Expressions

好美啊!　How beautiful it is!

反义 Antonym

美——丑　beautiful——ugly

幽默 Humor

好好当一天神仙吧。/我不是在做梦吧。
I want to be like a god for one day. / I am not dreaming.

联想 Association

张家界/九寨沟/香格里拉
Zhangjiajie/Jiuzhaigou/Shangerila

大自然的美景是无法用言语来形容的,必须身临其境去体验感受。

The beauty of nature can not be expressed by language. It must be sensed inside.

98

照相吗？
Zhàoxiàng ma?
Will you take a picture?

对话 Dialogue

A：照相吗？
　　Zhàoxiàng ma?　Will you take a picture?
B：好。
　　Hǎo.　All right.

类似说法 Similar Expressions

拍一张？　Do you want to have a picture taken?

幽默 Humor

我不想煞风景。　I do not want to disturb the scenery.

联想 Association

傻瓜机/数码相机/摄像机　　fool proof camera/digital camera/video camera

在美景中留影，或者把美景拍下来，都是旅游的一大乐趣。相机也变化真快，黑白的、彩色的、数码的，没有几年的时间，现在大部分人都用数码的了，胶卷都快卖不出去了。

It's one of the great pleasures of traveling to photograph or be photographed in the beautiful scenery. Great progress has been made in this area, from the old black and white camers, to color film, and now digital pictures. Many people are using digital cameras. Films is becoming a thing of the past.

99

谢谢。
Xièxie.
Thank you.

对话 Dialogue

A:照了!
　　Zhào le! Got it!
B:谢谢。
　　Xièxie. Thank you.

类似说法 Similar Expressions

笑一笑! /茄子! Smile/Qiezi (Eggplant)!

反义 Antonym

谢谢。——不谢。 Thank you. ——Don't mention it.

幽默 Humor

您会照相吗? You do know how to use a camera,
don't you?

联想 Association

照相/摄影/录像/绘画 to take a picture/to take a photo/
to video/to paint

现在,通常人们照相的时候爱说"茄子",因为说"茄子"时的口型和笑的时候一样。如果要请别人给照相,可以说"麻烦您",把照相机递给过路人就可以。

We usually say "qiezi" (eggplant) when taking pictures as it makes one look like they are smiling when saying it. If you want other people to take a picture for you, you may say "Excuse me" and offer him/her your camera.

100

去农家乐吧。
Qù nóngjiā lè ba.
Go to the Farmer's House.

对话 Dialogue

A: 天晚了。
Tiān wǎn le. It is late.

B: 去农家乐吧。
Qù nóngjiā lè ba. Let's go to the Farmer's House

类似说法 Similar Expressions

住农家乐。 to live in Farmer's House

反义 Antonym

农家乐——宾馆 to go to the Farmer's House——to go to a hotel

幽默 Humor

回归自然吧。 Let's go back to nature.

联想 Association

农村/农民 countryside/farmer

202

现在旅游流行去"农家乐"，就是住在农民家里，吃农村饭。城里人体验一下农民的生活，很有意思。农家乐也叫农家院、农家小院、民俗村。

Now it is popular to go to the "Farmer's House", meaning to live in farmer's home and eat their meals. City people are interested in what a farmer's life is like. Farmer's House is also called Farmer's Yard, Farmer's Courtyard or Folk-custom Village.

101

真香！
Zhēn xiāng!
It tastes savory!

对话 Dialogue

A:请喝粥。

Qǐng hē zhōu. Have some porridge please.

B:真香！

Zhēn xiāng! It tastes savory!

类似说法 Similar Expressions

味道好极了！ The flavor is excellent.

反义 Antonym

香——臭 fragrant——smelly

幽默 Humor

溜溜缝儿吧！ Fill the empty places of my full stomach.

联想 Association

小米粥/棒糙粥/粟米粥 millet congee/corn congee/
maize congee

农民用新粮食煮的粥特别香,您一定要多喝几碗。

The congee of the farmers consists of newly-harvested corn. You'd better try to have several bowls.

102

来点儿小菜。
Lái diǎnr xiǎocài.
Have some vegetable.

对话 Dialogue

A:来点儿小菜。

　　Lái diǎnr xiǎocài.　Have some side dish.

B:很好吃。

　　Hěn hǎo chī.　It's delicious.

类似说法 Similar Expressions

来点儿凉拌菜。　Have some cold dishes.

反义 Antonym

小菜——大菜　side dish——major course

幽默 Humor

这是中式沙拉。　This is Chinese-style salad.

联想 Association

来点儿干的。/来点儿鲜野菜。/来点儿刺激的。

Some solid food please. / Some fresh wild vegetable please. / Some hot and spicy dishes please.

206

吃饭要咸淡搭配，干稀搭配；光吃粥，嘴里没味儿，那就不好了。农村的山野菜可是绿色食品，味道鲜美，您可要多吃几口啊！

When eating meals, arrange different courses together, such as salty flavored one with a light one, solid food with soup. Congee is tasteless without vegetable. Fresh potherb in the country- side is green food and it tastes delicious. Have a try!

103

去过后海吗？
Qù guo Hòuhǎi ma?
Have you been to Houhai?

对话 Dialogue

A：去过后海吗？
Qù guo Hòuhǎi ma? Have you been to Houhai?
B：去过。
Qù guo. Yes, I have.

类似说法 Similar Expressions

去过什刹海吗？ Have you been to Shishahai?

反义 Antonym

后海——前海 back lake——front lake

幽默 Humor

天上人间。 Even though we are still in the real world, it feels like heaven.

联想 Association

三里屯酒吧一条街/后海酒吧一条街
Sanlitun Bar Street/Houhai Bar Street

208

北京原本没有夜生活,酒吧的兴起不过近十几年的事,水平自然不高,但是去逛一逛还是可以的。北京的酒吧一条街,以三里屯和后海最有名;后海后来居上,现在已经超过了三里屯。各国朋友很多,您可以抽时间去体验体验。

Formerly Beijing had no night life. Bars appeared only about ten years ago and are not highly developed, but it is still worth visiting some. The most famous bars are around the Sanlitun and Houhai districts. Bars in the Houhai district now are better than the ones in Sanlitun. There are often many foreign friends there. You may go around to have a drink.

104

感觉特好。
Gǎnjué tè hǎo.
I feel great.

对话 Dialogue

A:怎么样?
　Zěnmeyàng?　How do you feel?
B:感觉特好。
　Gǎnjué tè hǎo.　I feel great.

类似说法 Similar Expressions

感觉特别棒!　I feel terrific!

反义 Antonym

特好——没劲　great——depressed

幽默 Humor

赛过活神仙!　I am living more pleasantly than an immortal.

联想 Association

找刺激/找清净/找情调/放松一下
to seek an incentive/a quiet place/a taste/to relax

酒吧里独有一种惬意和闲适,那不是每个人都能感觉到并且享受得了的。花点酒水钱,买的是个舒坦。

The comfort and relaxation found in bars may not be appreciated by everyone or within everyone's budget. Here you spend some money to buy a kind of relaxed feeling.

105

我们今天去?
Wǒmen jīntiān qù?
Shall we go today?

对话 Dialogue

A:我们今天去?

　　Wǒmen jīntiān qù?　Shall we go today?

B:好。

　　Hǎo.　Sure.

类似说法 Similar Expressions

现在就走! /说走就走!　Let's go! / To go on a whim!

反义 Antonym

去——不去　go——do not go

幽默 Humor

择日不如撞日。　To choose an auspicious day is inferior to meeting it by coincidence.

联想 Association

明天/后天/昨天　tomorrow/the day after tomorrow/ yesterday

"说走就走"是一种很有意思的做法,心理基础是按照兴趣行事,有兴趣才有感觉,有感觉才有意思。

"To go on a whim" is an interesting way of doing something. It refers to do something according to one's own interest.

106

太好了!
Tài hǎo le!
It is great!

对话 Dialogue

A: 环境怎么样?

Huánjìng zěnmeyàng?　What do you think of the environment?

B: 太好了!

Tài hǎo le!　It is great!

类似说法 Similar Expressions

真棒!　It is terrific!

反义 Antonym

太好了! —— 不怎么样。　It is terrific! —— It is just so so.

幽默 Humor

没治了。　It is the extreme.

联想 Association

酒吧/茶吧/咖啡吧　bar/tea bar/cafe

后海所以能够后来居上,是因为它的酒吧围湖而建;坐在酒吧里,一边喝着饮料,一边还可以欣赏湖光水色,确实别有一番风味! 另外您还可以在湖边漫步,在湖中荡舟。

The more recent bars opened in Houhai surpass those found in Sanlitun because they are built around the lake. It is really enjoyable to have a drink while having a view of the lake! Besides you may walk around the lake and boat on it.

107

京戏票。
Jīngxì piào.
It is a ticket for Peking Opera.

对话 Dialogue

A：什么票？
Shénme piào?　What is it for?

B：京戏票。
Jīngxì piào.　It is a ticket for Peking Opera.

类似说法 Similar Expressions

京戏入场券　entrance ticket for Peking Opera

幽默 Humor

彩票　lottery ticket

联想 Association

京剧/舞剧/歌剧/音乐剧
Peking Opera/pantomime/opera/melodrama

京戏是中国的国粹,讲究唱、念、做、打,具有极强的虚拟性,值得一看。

Peking Opera is the national opera of China. It combines singing, acting, dancing and fighting. It is very imaginative and worth experiencing.

108

是武戏，挺热闹。
Shì wǔ xì, tǐng rènao.
This is about warriors and fighting,
it is very exciting.

对话 Dialogue

A: 好看吗？

　Hǎo kàn ma?　Is it interesting?

B: 是武戏，挺热闹。

　Shì wǔ xì, tǐng rènao.　This is about warriors and fighting, it is very exciting.

类似说法 Similar Expressions

是武打的。　It is a play about fighting.

反义 Antonym

武戏——文戏　military play——literary play

幽默 Humor

外行看热闹。　People who do not understand the meaning only enjoy the excitement.

联想 Association

生/旦/净/末/丑　sheng-leading male actor/ dan-female role/ jing-male painted-face role/ mo-minor old-male role / chou-comic role——five main roles in Peking Opera

一般不懂中文的各国朋友看京剧都是从武戏看起，这就是俗话说的"看热闹"。要是你真想看懂文戏，那一是要会点儿中文，二是要了解点儿文化历史背景。

Foreigners who do not know Chinese will appreciate Peking Opera more for its military-style action, being entertained by "watching the excitement" on the stage. If you really want to watch a dramatic play, you must first know some Chinese and understand its cultural and historical background.

真不错!
Zhēn búcuò!
It is really good!

对话 Dialogue

A:真不错!
Zhēn búcuò! It is really good!
B:好!
Hǎo! Great!

类似说法 Similar Expressions

太棒了! It is terrific!

反义 Antonym

真不错! ——真没劲! It is really good! ——It is really boring!

幽默 Humor

我也要上去露一手! I also want to show my skills on the stage!

联想 Association

武术/散打/柔道/跆拳道 martial art/ brawl fight/ judo/ kickboxing

艺术是相通的,艺术是世界性的,相信您一定会被中国的国粹剧所感动。在您表示赞赏时,可以大声喊"好!"这是老北京人看京戏时的习惯,"叫好"这个词就是这么来的。

Art is a kind of universal communication. We believe you will be moved by our national opera. To express your appreciation, you may shout "Good". This is customarily done by old Peking Opera fans. The phrase "Shouting Good" comes from this tradition.

110

看球吗?
Kàn qiú ma?
Do you want to watch a game?

对话 Dialogue

A: 看球吗?
　　Kàn qiú ma?　Do you want to watch a game?

B: 看!
　　Kàn!　Of course!

类似说法 Similar Expressions

看不看球赛?　Do you want to watch a game or not?

反义 Antonym

看——不看　to watch——not to watch

幽默 Humor

我去了准输。　They will definitely lose the game if I go.

联想 Association

看体操/看田径/看游泳/看跳水
To watch gym/track and field/swimming/diving

　　各种体育迷中,数足球迷最酷。为什么足球有那么大的魅力呢? 天知道! 反正几万人一齐呐喊的场景实在让人振奋。可惜中国的足球这几年太臭,有时现场观众加上警察才上千人。

Among the many different sports fans, football fans are the coolest. Why is football so attractive? God knows! Thousands of people shout together and it is really an exciting spectacle. Unfortunately, interest in Chinese football has recently been at low tide, there have been only a thousand spectators at each game, including the policemen.

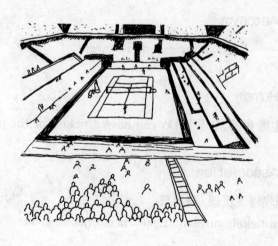

111

要票吗?
Yào piào ma?
Do you want a ticket?

对话 Dialogue

A: 要票吗?
　　Yào piào ma?　Do you want a ticket?
B: 不要。
　　Bú yào.　No, I don't.

类似说法 Similar Expressions

看球吗?　Do you want to watch a game?

反义 Antonym

要——不要　want——do not want

幽默 Humor

有主席台的票吗?　Do you have a ticket for the podium?

联想 Association

火车票/飞机票/演出票
train ticket/ airplane ticket/performance ticket

224

贴心提示 Tips

票贩子的票能买吗？千万别买。一是可能贵，二是可能假。出了问题你再找他可就找不着了。

Should you buy tickets from individuals selling tickets on the street—ticket scalpers? Surely you should not. The tickets are most probably expensive or fake. Moreover, in case there is a problem, you can never find them.

加油！
Jiāyóu!
Go!

对话 Dialogue

A:加油！
  Jiāyóu!　Go!
B:加油！
  Jiāyóu!　Come on!

类似说法 Similar Expressions

雄起！　Let's fight!

幽默 Humor

失败是胜利的妈妈。　Defeat is the mother of victory.

联想 Association

冲啊！/豁出去了！/拼了！
Charge! /Let's fight! /Fight to the finish!

226

中国有句古话:胜败乃兵家常事。还有一句古话:不以成败论英雄。奥林匹克的口号是:重在参与。所以,输赢是暂时的,友谊是永恒的。胜了别骄傲,败了别气馁。在看台上要多为双方运动员鼓掌加油,以显示您的水平和风度!

There is an old Chinese saying which states that, winning or losing a battle is a common occurrence. Another saying reminds us not to judge a hero according to his success or failure. The slogan of the Olympic Games is that participation is the most important thing. To win or to lose is a temporary situation, but the friendship you make during the competition will last forever. Don't be proud when you win and don't be depressed when you lose. Please applaud for both the wining and losing athletes to show your sportsmanship and good manners!

去洗浴中心吗？
Qù xǐyù zhōngxīn ma?
Do you want to go to a public bathhouse?

对话 Dialogue

A: 去洗浴中心吗？

   Qù xǐyù zhōngxīn ma?　Do you want to go to a public bathhouse?

B: 去。

   Qù.　Yes, I do.

类似说法 Similar Expressions

洗澡去？/桑拿去？　take a bath? / take a sauna bath?

反义 Antonym

洗澡吗？——不洗。　Do you take a bath? —— No, I don't.

幽默 Humor

天天洗澡，把皮都洗掉了！　If you take a bath every day you will wash off your skin!

联想 Association

澡堂/浴池/蒸气浴/水浴　bathhouse/bathing pool/steam bath/water bath

韩国有个电视剧《澡堂老板家的男人们》在中国的收视率很高,可见到外面去洗澡是各国朋友都愿意享受的一种乐趣。当您游览了一天,又累又乏时,泡个澡,按摩按摩,疲劳顿时一扫而光!

There is a Korean teleplay called Men of the Bathhouse Boss's Family, which enjoys a high viewing rate in China. You can see that to bathe in a public bathhouse is a pleasure for people of the world. If you feel tired and exhausted after a day's sightseeing, a warm bath and massage might be a good way to reenergize yourself!

您好！请进！
Nín hǎo! Qǐng jìn!
How do you do! Come in please!

对话 Dialogue

A: 您好！请进！
Nín hǎo! Qǐng jìn!　How do you do! Come in please!
B: 您好。
Nín hǎo.　How do you do!

类似说法 Similar Expressions

欢迎光临！/来啦，几位？　Welcome! /Nice to meet you,
how many people?

反义 Antonym

进——出　in——out

幽默 Humor

把这儿当家啦？　You are acting as if this is your own
home.

联想 Association

蒸桑拿/按摩/足疗　to take sauna bath/to have a mas-
sage/to do a foot massage

230

"您好! 请进!"等是服务员打招呼的常用语。也有的说 "来啦,几位?"

"How do you do! Come in please!" is a customary greeting by the attendants. Some may also add, "Nice to meet you, how many people?"

喝点儿什么?
Hē diǎnr shénme?
What would you like to drink?

对话 Dialogue

A:喝点儿什么?
Hē diǎnr shénme? What would you like to drink?
B:白开水。
Bái kāi shuǐ. Water please.

类似说法 Similar Expressions

来点儿什么喝的? Do you want something to drink?

反义 Antonym

喝——吃 drink——eat

幽默 Humor

喝不要钱的水。 I just want to drink something free.

联想 Association

矿泉水/纯净水/果汁
boiled water/mineral water/purified water/fruit juice

　　洗完澡后客人要休息一下,老板方面提供饮料、点心、正餐等服务。

After bathing, guests may need to have a rest. The manager will provide drinks, snacks and meals.

116

力度怎么样？

Lìdù zěnmeyàng?

How do you feel about the intensity?

对话 Dialogue

A：力度怎么样？

Lìdù zěnmeyàng?　How do you feel about the intensity?

B：再轻点儿。

Zài qīng diǎnr.　Less intense please.

类似说法 Similar Expressions

这个强度行吗？　Is this pressure okay?

反义 Antonym

轻点儿——重点儿　less intense——more intense

幽默 Humor

你是不是想要我的命呀？　Are you trying to kill me?

联想 Association

踩背/推油/泰式/港式　step on the back/rub with oil/
Thai-style/Hong Kong-style

234

洗澡后，一般人都要按摩，"力度怎么样"是服务人员用来询问用劲儿大小、轻重的常用语。如果您觉得用劲儿大了，可以说"再轻点儿"。

Massage is often done after a bath. "How do you feel about the intensity?" is often used by the masseur to ask about the pressure of the massage. If you feel it is too intense, you may say "less intense please."

再重点儿！
Zài zhòng diǎnr!
More intense please!

对话 Dialogue

A: 力度够吗？
Lìdù gòu ma? What do you think of the intensity?
B: 再重点儿！
Zài zhòng diǎnr! More intense please!

类似说法 Similar Expressions

再使点劲儿！ More pressure please!

反义 Antonym

重点儿——轻点儿 more intense——more gentle

幽默 Humor

您没吃饭吗？ Haven't you eaten your meals?

联想 Association

放松/舒服/疼/酸 to be relaxed/comfortable/ painful/ sore

如果您觉得没什么感觉，可以说"再重点儿"。

If you think the massage is too gentle, you may say "more intense please ."

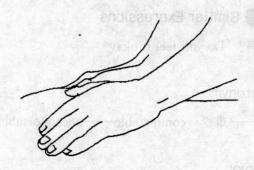

118

感觉怎么样？
Gǎnjué zěnmeyàng?
How do you feel?

对话 Dialogue

A:感觉怎么样？
 Gǎnjué zěnmeyàng?　How do you feel?

B:很舒服。
 Hěn shūfu.　Quite comfortable.

类似说法 Similar Expressions

还行吗？　Do you feel it okay?

反义 Antonym

舒服——难受　comfortable——uncomfortable

幽默 Humor

飘飘欲仙。　I am feeling just like an immortal.

如果您觉得服务生用的力量合适，可以说"很舒服"，表示您对服务生满意。

If you feel the intensity of the massage is appropriate, you may say "quite comfortable" to express your satisfaction.

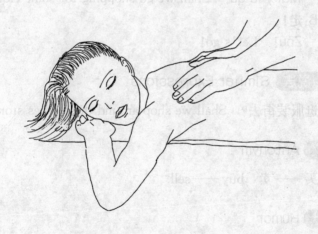

买东西
mǎi dōngxi **Shopping**

119

买衣服去?
Mǎi yīfu qù?
Shall we go shopping for some clothes?

对话 Dialogue

A:买衣服去?
  Mǎi yīfu qù? Shall we go shopping for some clothes?
B:走!
  Zǒu! Let's go!

类似说法 Similar Expressions

逛服装街去? Shall we shop around the clothes stores?

反义 Antonym

买——卖 buy——sell

幽默 Humor

该换行头了。 It is time to change your acting costumes.

联想 Association

上衣/衬衫/裤子/裙子 jacket/shirt/trousers/skirt

俗话说"衣食住行",可见衣服是第一重要的。三里屯一带的雅秀服装市场,是享誉中外的,小威廉姆斯来中国打球时,还光顾过呢! 此外双榆树西里服饰一条街、双安商场西侧北京科技会展中心1、2、3层的服饰小店、东四服饰一条街等等,都还可以。相信您能在北京的小店里,买到自己满意的服饰。

We usually mention "clothes, food, housing and traffic", but clothes takes first place. Yaxiu Clothes Markets around Sanlitun is known around the world. Williams Junior once visited it when coming to play tennis in China! Other places are not bad either, such as the clothes stalls on the street of Shuangyushu Xili, boutiques on the 1st, 2nd and 3rd floors of the Beijing Science Convention Center west of Shuang'an Market, and the small clothes stores of Dongsi. We are sure that you will have a satisfying shopping experience in the clothes shops of Beijing.

看点儿什么？
Kàn diǎnr shénme?
What do you want?

120

对话 Dialogue

A:看点儿什么？

　　Kàn diǎnr shénme?　What do you want?

B:随便看看。

　　Suíbiàn kànkan.　We are just looking.

类似说法 Similar Expressions

需要点儿什么？/喜欢什么？/买什么？

Can I help you? /Do you have anything in mind? /What
are you looking for?

反义 Antonym

看——不看　want——don't want

联想 Association

西服/衬衫/T 恤/牛仔裤　suit/shirt/T-shirt/jeans

121

我试试这个。
Wǒ shìshi zhè ge.
I'd like to try this on.

对话 Dialogue

A:我试试这个。

Wǒ shìshi zhè ge.　I'd like to try this on.

B:给您。

Gěi nín.　Here you are.

类似说法 Similar Expressions

喜欢哪件可以试穿。　You may try on whatever you like.

反义 Antonym

试试——不能试　try on——do not try on

幽默 Humor

我是衣服架子。　I am just like a clothes model.

联想 Association

穿衣/戴帽/照镜子　to dress/wear a cap/look into the mirror

244

贴心提示 Tips

买衣服必须要试穿，挂在那儿好看，穿在您身上不一定好看。如果卖主不让您试，您就别再理会他了，因为卖家有的是。

When buying clothes, one must try it on because sometimes it looks nice but does not fit. If the seller does not allow you to try a piece of clothing on, you may have a go to other markets where you are permitted to try things on.

这件多少钱?
Zhè jiàn duōshǎo qián?
How much is this?

对话 Dialogue

A：这件多少钱?
　　Zhè jiàn duōshǎo qián?　How much is this?
B：200。
　　Èrbǎi.　200.

类似说法 Similar Expressions

这件怎么卖?　What is the price for this one?

反义 Antonym

这——那　this——that

幽默 Humor

这件您买不起。　You can't afford it.

联想 Association

一件衬衫/一条裤子/一套西服　a shirt/trousers/a suit

如果您相中了哪件，试穿后感觉不错，想买下来的时候，就说这句话。如果根本不想买，就不要问价钱。

If you like it and feel good after trying it on, you may ask the price. If you do not like it, do not bother to ask about the price.

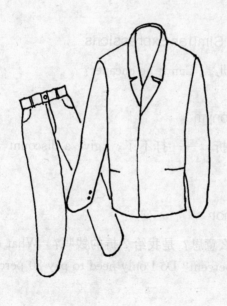

123

打点儿折吧。
Dǎ diǎnr zhé ba.
Please give a discount.

对话 Dialogue

A: 打点儿折吧。

　　Dǎ diǎnr zhé ba.　Please give a discount.

B: 给您打 8 折。

　　Gěi nín dǎ bā zhé.　20 percent for you.

类似说法 Similar Expressions

便宜点儿。　Can it be cheaper?

反义 Antonym

打点儿折。——打不了。　give a discount —— It's set price.

幽默 Humor

8 折什么意思？是我给 2 折的钱吗？　What do you mean by 20 percent? Do I only need to pay 20 percent?

联想 Association

砍价/杀价　to negotiate price/to bargain for a lower price

这是砍价时的常用语。一般的服饰小店，都可以砍价，俗话说"见面砍一半"。

This is often used to negotiate the prices. In ordinary boutiques you can always bargain with the seller. There is a popular phrase used in this process that asks the seller to "cut the prices by half".

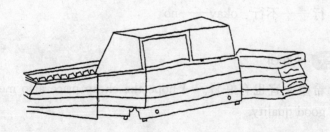

124

行，给您钱。
Xíng, gěi nín qián.
Okay, here is the money.

对话 Dialogue

A:行，给您钱。
Xíng, gěi nín qián.　Okay, here is the money.
B:您拿好。
Nín ná hǎo.　Take it please.

类似说法 Similar Expressions

好吧，我要了。　Okay, I'll take it.

反义 Antonym

行——不行　okay——no

幽默 Humor

希望便宜也有好货。　I hope the cheap price also means good quality.

联想 Association

物美价廉/物有所值　be of good quality and best price/be worth the prices charged

这是您觉得可以买下来时说的话,萝卜、白菜各有所爱,只要您喜欢就值。如果您不喜欢,再便宜也没用。

That an item is 'worth it' may be said by you when you decide to buy it. Everyone will like things of their own taste. If you like it, you get good value for money. If you do not, it is of no value.

125

这鞋有 38 的吗？
Zhè xié yǒu sān bā de ma?
Do you have size 38 in these shoes?

对话 Dialogue

A：这鞋有 38 的吗？
Zhè xié yǒu sān bā de ma?　Do you have size 38 in these shoes?

B：有。
Yǒu.　Yes, we have.

类似说法 Similar Expressions

这鞋有我穿的吗？　Do you have the shoes in my size?

反义 Antonym

有——没有　have——do not have

幽默 Humor

这是灰姑娘的鞋，没号。These are Cinderella's shoes, no size.

联想 Association

38 号/39 号/24 号/25 号　size 38/39/24/25

买鞋一定要自己试,不能请别人代买。因为有时候同样号码的大小和肥瘦不太一样。

To buy shoes you'd better try them on yourself instead of asking other people to buy them for you as sometimes the length and width of shoes marked as being the same size are different.

126

大了点儿。
Dà le diǎnr.
It's a bit bigger.

对话 Dialogue

> A: 给您。
>
> Gěi nín. Here you are.
>
> B: 大了点儿。
>
> Dà le diǎnr. It's a bit bigger.

类似说法 Similar Expressions

> 有点儿大。 It's slightly bigger.

反义 Antonym

> 大——小 big——small

幽默 Humor

> 成小船儿了。 It's like a boat.

联想 Association

> 元宝鞋/懒汉鞋/一带鞋 yuanbao cloth shoes/lanhan
> cloth shoes/one-ribbon shoes

贴心提示 Tips

　　来到中国您一定要买一双手工做的布鞋,穿着非常舒服。老字号有:内联升、步瀛斋等。如果您觉得老字号的鞋贵,也可以到百货批发城或者农村的集市上去买,不过要仔细挑选,注意质量。

　　We suggest you buy a pair of hand-made cloth shoes in China because they are very comfortable. Old stores are Neiliansheng, Buyingzhai and etc. If you think their prices are high, indoor wholesale markets or open country markets also sell these shoes. Please take a good look at the quality before you buy.

有点儿小。
Yǒu diǎnr xiǎo.
A bit small.

对话 Dialogue

A:这个怎么样？
 Zhè ge zěnmeyàng?   How is it?
B:有点儿小。
 Yǒu diǎnr xiǎo.   A bit small.

类似说法 Similar Expressions

有点儿夹脚。   They hurt.

反义 Antonym

 小 —— 大   small —— big

幽默 Humor

 是我的脚太大了！ It is my big feet which do not suit the
 shoes!

联想 Association

 有点儿窄。/有点儿紧。   a bit narrow/a bit tight

　　买鞋您一定要试好,穿上以后多走几步,确实合适了再买。

To buy shoes, you'd better try them on and walk a few steps to see if they fit.

128

很舒服。
Hěn shūfu.
It suits me well.

To buy shoes, you'd better try them on and walk
a few steps to see if they fit.

对话 Dialogue

> A：试试这个。
>
> Shìshi zhè ge.　Try it on.
>
> B：很舒服。
>
> Hěn shūfu.　It suits me well.

类似说法 Similar Expressions

正合适。　It's a good fit.

反义 Antonym

舒服——不合适　comfortable——do not fit

幽默 Humor

穿上跟没穿似的。　Wearing them is just like wearing
nothing.

联想 Association

布鞋/皮鞋/球鞋/拖鞋　cloth shoes/leather shoes/sports
shoes/slipper

鞋穿舒服了，您的心情也自然愉快。

Wearing comfortable shoes can make you feel happy.

要古玩吗?
Yào gǔwán ma?
Do you want some antiques?

对话 Dialogue

A:要古玩吗?

　Yào gǔwán ma?　Do you want some antiques?

B:怎么卖?

　Zěnme mài?　How much is it?

类似说法 Similar Expressions

买几件古玩吧? /看点儿什么?　Will you buy some antiques? /What are you looking for?

反义 Antonym

古──今　ancient──modern

幽默 Humor

有做旧的吗?　Do you have anything fake?

联想 Association

玉器/青铜器/陶器/字画　jade article/bronzeware/
keramics/calligraphy and painting

北京的古玩市场有:潘家园、红桥等。潘家园每周六、日才开,各国朋友很多;您如果对古玩感兴趣,可以去看看,非常热闹。说不定还能淘到点儿金呢!

Antiques markets in Beijing are mainly Panjiayuan Market and Hongqiao Market. Panjiayuan Market is only open on Saturdays and Sundays and it attracts many international friends. If you are interested in antiques, you should go to have a look. You might find some unusual things!

130

太贵了！
Tài guì le!
It's so expensive!

对话 Dialogue

A：1000。
Yì qiān. 1000.

B：太贵了！
Tài guì le! It's so expensive!

类似说法 Similar Expressions

这么贵啊？ How expensive it is!

反义 Antonym

贵——贱 expensive——cheap

幽默 Humor

您开玩笑吧？ Are you kidding?

联想 Association

1500/2000/3000

在古玩市场是可以砍价的，"太贵"是砍价时的常用语。

In antiques markets you may bargain with the seller and "it is too expensive" is a common phrase used to begin the negotiations.

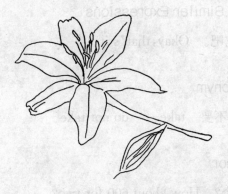

131

我要了。
Wǒ yào le.
I'll take it.

对话 Dialogue

A：600。
　　Liùbǎi.　600.
B：我要了。
　　Wǒ yào le.　I'll take it.

类似说法 Similar Expressions

行，就它吧。　Okay, that's it.

反义 Antonym

要——不要　take——do not take

幽默 Humor

600 两个？　How about 600 for two?

联想 Association

100/200/500/700

"我要了"的意思就是接受这个价钱,决定买下。砍价时要有耐心,不要轻易让步。砍价还要有信心,当然这信心来自您的眼光。

"I will take it" means you accept this price and decide to buy it. When negotiating prices, one needs to be patient and persistent. Confidence based on your good sense is also a must when bargaining with the seller.

去超市。
Qù chāo shì.
Go to the supermarket.

对话 Dialogue

A:没有饼干了。
　　Méiyǒu bǐnggān le.　We do not have any biscuits left.
B:去超市。
　　Qù chāo shì.　Go to the supermarket.

类似说法 Similar Expressions

去自选商场。　Go to the self-service store.

反义 Antonym

超市──不能自选的商店
supermarket──department store

幽默 Humor

有超市就有一切。　With supermarkets we get all we
need.

联想 Association

面包/黄油/果酱　bread/butter/jam

266

最近几年,大大小小的超市布满了中国的大街小巷,买食品、日用品非常方便。

Recently, both large and small supermarkets have opened on almost every street. They make the daily purchases of food and routine products very convenient.

133

前边右手。
Qiánbiān yòushǒu.
Straight ahead and to your right.

对话 Dialogue

A：请问饼干在哪儿？

Qǐngwèn bǐnggān zài nǎr? Can you tell me where I can buy biscuits?

B：前边右手。

Qiánbiān yòushǒu. Straight ahead and to your right.

类似说法 Similar Expressions

往前走，再往右拐。 Go ahead and turn to the right.

反义 Antonym

前——后 ahead——behind

幽默 Humor

右边的手上？ Is it really ON my right hand?

联想 Association

上/下/左/中 above/under/left/middle

大超市的商品琳琅满目,您如果找不到需要的东西,向服务员询问比较省时间。

It is difficult to look for a certain commodity in big supermarkets. If you can not find it, asking an assistant for help can save you a lot of time.

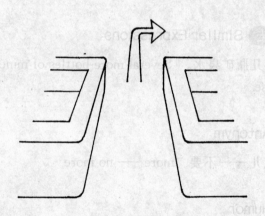

134

再来点儿水。
Zài lái diǎnr shuǐ.
More water, please.

对话 Dialogue

A:再来点儿水。
　　Zài lái diǎnr shuǐ.　More water, please.
B:行。
　　Xíng.　Okay.

类似说法 Similar Expressions

再买几瓶矿泉水。　Several more bottles of mineral water please.

反义 Antonym

来点儿——不要　more——no more

幽默 Humor

喝自来水就行了。　It is okay we drink the tap water.

联想 Association

饮料/可口可乐/果汁　drink/Coke/fruit juice

超市的饮料都很便宜，质量也有保证，您可以多买一些，外出旅游时带上。

Drinks sold in supermarket are cheap and of good quality. You may buy more to take with you when going out.

135

水果也不错。
Shuǐguǒ yě búcuò.
The fruit is not bad either.

对话 Dialogue

A：水果也不错。

　　Shuǐguǒ yě búcuò.　The fruit is not bad either.

B：也拿点儿。

　　Yě ná diǎnr.　Take some.

类似说法 Similar Expressions

水果挺好的。　The fruit is excellent.

反义 Antonym

不错——不好　not bad——not good

幽默 Humor

你付钱就都拿上。　If you pay, I will take all these.

联想 Association

柠檬/提子/火龙果/芒果　lemon/grape/dragon fruit/ginseng fruit

超市的水果不一定便宜，也不一定新鲜，您可要仔细挑选！

Fruit in the supermarkets is not always cheap and fresh. You must choose carefully!

136

找您 3 块。
Zhǎo nín sān kuài.
Here is your 3 yuan change.

对话 Dialogue

A:97 块,给您 100。
Jiǔshíqī kuài, gěi nín yìbǎi. 97 yuan, here is 100 yuan.

B:找您 3 块。
Zhǎo nín sān kuài. Here is your 3 yuan change.

类似说法 Similar Expressions

收您 100 块,找您 20 块。 You paid 100, this is your 20 yuan change.

反义 Antonym

找您。——正好,不找了。 your change——no change

联想 Association

卫生纸/袜子/背心/牛奶/薯片/巧克力
toilet paper/stockings/vest/milk/potato chips/chocolate

超市都使用电子收银机,如果您没听清楚报价,可以看显示器。如果您买的东西多,可以用超市提供的小车推出去。

Cash registers are used in supermarkets. If you do not quite hear the prices, you may look at the display screen for the amount you are being charged.

您买什么茶?
Nín mǎi shénme chá?
What kind of tea do you want?

对话 Dialogue

A: 您买什么茶?

　　Nín mǎi shénme chá?　What kind of tea do you want?

B: 红茶。

　　Hóngchá.　Black tea.

类似说法 Similar Expressions

需要哪种茶?　What kind of tea would you prefer?

反义 Antonym

买——卖　buy——sell

幽默 Humor

我都先尝尝行吗?　Can I taste all of them first?

联想 Association

龙井/碧螺春/毛尖/毛峰/大红袍

Longjing tea/Biluochun tea/Maojian tea/Maofeng tea/Dahongpao tea

贴心提示 Tips

　　买茶最好到老字号茶店，比如"张一元"。茶叶分三大类：绿茶、红茶、乌龙茶。不发酵的是绿茶，全发酵的是红茶，半发酵的是乌龙茶。花茶是用茉莉花熏的，茶农不喝花茶。

　　中国的名茶有：西湖龙井、洞庭碧螺春、信阳毛尖、君山银针、六安瓜片、黄山毛峰、祁门红茶、庐山云雾、安溪铁观音、武夷岩茶等，您可以品尝以后购买您喜欢喝的那种。

To buy tea you'd better go to the old brand stores, such as Zhangyiyuan. The three main categories of tea are green , black, and oolong. Green tea is steamed to stop oxidation, black tea is fermented for hours, and oolong tea is partially fermented. Jasmine Tea is scented with jasmine flower essence, and the tea farmers never drink this kind of tea. Famous Chinese teas are: Xihu Longjing tea, Dongting Biluochun tea, Xinyang Maojian tea, Junshan Yinzhen tea, Liu'an Guapian tea, Huangshan Maofeng tea, Qimen black tea, Lushan Yunwu tea, Anxi Tieguanyin tea, and Wuyi Yan tea. You may drink to taste and then buy what you like the best.

您要多少钱 1 斤的?
Nín yào duōshǎo qián yì jīn de?
How much would you like to spend?

对话 Dialogue

A:您要多少钱 1 斤的?
　Nín yào duōshǎo qián yì jīn de?　How much would you like to spend?

B:300 的。
　Sānbǎi de.　300 yuan.

类似说法 Similar Expressions

您想花多少钱?　How much do you spend on tea?

反义 Antonym

要钱——免费　sale——free

幽默 Humor

我要物美价廉的。I want something of good quality and reasonable price.

联想 Association

200 块/400 块/500 块　200 yuan/400 yuan/500 yuan

278

像龙井茶贵的 1 斤要好几万元。一般人也就喝几百块钱的。您可以根据您的经济实力,在各档价格范围内选购。

If one takes Longjing Tea as an example, the most expensive would cost more than a million yuan per jin. Ordinary people may drink teas worth only several hundreds yuan per jin. You should purchase teas according to your own economic situation.

139 要多少?
Yào duōshǎo?
How much do you want?

对话 Dialogue

A: 要多少?
　　Yào duōshǎo?　How much do you want?
B: 100 克。
　　Yìbǎi kè.　100 grams.

类似说法 Similar Expressions

买多少?　How much would you like to buy?

反义 Antonym

多——少　much——little

幽默 Humor

我在北京呆两天,两天需要喝多少?　I will stay in Beijing for two days, how much do I need to drink?

联想 Association

1两/半斤/1斤　one liang/half jin/one jin

自己喝,一般一次买 250 克(半市斤),比较贵的可以买 50 克(1 两)试试。茶叶过期就不好喝了,所以一次不要买多了,喝完了再买。如果您自己喝,就用茶叶店特制的纸包好,拿回家再装到茶叶桶里。如果送朋友,可以挑选您喜欢的茶叶桶,这也是展示您审美观的机会哦!

We usually buy 250 grams (half a jin) for ourselves. As for expensive teas, we will buy 50 grams (one liang) in order to try it out. When tea gets too old, it tastes bad. So you'd better not buy too much. If you just buy for yourself, you may have it wrapped in a piece of paper by the tea shop and then put it into a sealed caddy at home. If you are buying for a friend, you may choose a nice tea caddy to go with the tea .

140 您买什么药?
Nín mǎi shénme yào?
What medicine do you want to buy?

对话 Dialogue

A:您买什么药?
Nín mǎi shénme yào?
What medicine do you want to buy?

B:感冒药。
Gǎnmào yào.　Medicine for a cold.

类似说法 Similar Expressions

感冒清热颗粒　anti-cold granule

反义 Antonym

买——不买　buy——do not buy

幽默 Humor

有长生不死药吗?　Do you have any medicine that can make me live forever?

联想 Association

头痛/发烧/咳嗽　headache/fever/cough

中国的传统中药店"同仁堂"最有名,其中治疗感冒的"感冒清热颗粒"效果非常好,受到各国朋友欢迎。

Tong Ren Tang is the most famous Traditional Chinese Medicine Manufacturer. Its "anti - cold granule" is very effective and popular with the people all over the world.

141

您要几盒?
Nín yào jǐ hé?
How many packs do you want?

对话 Dialogue

A: 您要几盒?
　　Nín yào jǐ hé?　How many packs do you want?
B: 1盒。
　　Yì hé.　One.

类似说法 Similar Expressions

您买多少?　How many do you want?

幽默 Humor

有多少要多少。　I shall take all you have.

联想 Association

板蓝根颗粒/感冒冲剂　Banlangen Granule/Anti‑cold
Granule

贴心提示 Tips

"感冒清热颗粒"1盒里有10袋,可以吃5天,感冒大概也就好了。药不宜多买,过期失效。

There are 10 small bags in one pack of anti-cold granule and this should last you for five days. Do not buy too much medicine as its effectivenss lessens as it ages.

142

水果新鲜吗?
Shuǐguǒ xīnxian ma?
Is the fruit fresh?

对话 Dialogue

A:水果新鲜吗?
　　Shuǐguǒ xīnxian ma?　Is the fruit fresh?
B:刚进的。
　　Gāng jìn de.　It has just been delivered.

类似说法 Similar Expressions

水果是刚来的吗?　Did the fruit just come?

反义 Antonym

新鲜——烂　fresh——rotten

幽默 Humor

刚从树上摘下来的。　I just picked them from the tree.

联想 Association

本地水果/外地水果/进口水果
local fruits/fruits from other places/fruits from other
countries

286

大超市虽然也有水果,但还是农贸市场的比较物美价廉,有些当地产的又新鲜又便宜。

Although there is fruit available in supermarkets, fruit in open markets is more reasonably priced and are fresher and cheaper, especially those produced locally.

143 怎么卖?
Zěnme mài?
How much?

对话 Dialogue

A: 怎么卖?
Zěnme mài?　How much?

B: 3块。
Sān kuài.　3 yuan.

类似说法 Similar Expressions

10块钱3斤/1斤3块　10 yuan for 3 jin/ 3 yuan for 1 jin

反义 Antonym

卖——买　sell——buy

幽默 Humor

尝几个行吗?　Can I taste some?

联想 Association

梨/苹果/香蕉/橙子　pear/apple/banana/orange

买水果不要太图便宜,俗话说"宁吃鲜桃一口,不吃烂桃一筐"。

Do not make cheap prices your main concern. There is a saying that should remind of this which states, "I'd rather eat a mouthful of fresh peach than a basket of rotten peaches".

144

够了吗？

Gòu le ma?

Are these enough?

对话 Dialogue

A: 够了吗？

　　Gòu le ma?　Are these enough?

B: 够了。

　　Gòu le.　Enoug h.

类似说法 Similar Expressions

再来点儿。　More please.

反义 Antonym

够了——不够　enough——not enough

幽默 Humor

够我吃半年了！　It is enough to last me for half a year!

联想 Association

葡萄/桃/杏/草莓　grape/peach/apricot/strawberry

贴心提示 Tips

这是卖主希望您再多买一些时说的话。您能吃多少就买多少，千万不要被老板的热情感动，水果烂了就没法吃了。

This is often said by the seller who hopes that you will buy more. You should just buy as much or as little as you wish. Do not be tempted by the seller as fruit can not be kept for long and they go bad quickly.

要鲜花吗?

Yào xiānhuā ma?

Do you want some flowers?

对话 Dialogue

A:要鲜花吗?

Yào xiānhuā ma?　Do you want some flowers?

B:看看。

Kànkan.　I am just looking.

类似说法 Similar Expressions

买鲜花吗? /喜欢什么花?　Would you like to buy some flowers? / Which flower do you prefer?

反义 Antonym

鲜——枯　fresh flower——dried flower

幽默 Humor

能老活着吗?　Can it be fresh forever?

联想 Association

玫瑰/百合/康乃馨/郁金香　rose/lily/carnation/tulip

花市里，卖鲜插花的爱招揽顾客，如果您不买，可到盆花摊位那边去看看。

In the flower market, sellers of cut fresh flowers tend to attract customers. If you do not want to buy, you may just go to have a look at the potted flowers.

这花特香！
Zhè huā tè xiāng!
This flower smells very sweet!

对话 Dialogue

A：这花特香！
　　Zhè huā tè xiāng!　This flower smells very sweet!
B：是吗？
　　Shì ma?　Really?

类似说法 Similar Expressions

这种特别香！　This kind smells extremely sweet!

反义 Antonym

香——臭　sweet——smelly

幽默 Humor

比香水还香吗？　Is it sweeter than perfume?

联想 Association

水仙/米兰/蝴蝶兰/杜鹃/绿萝/仙人球
narcissus/freesia/butterfly orchid/azalea/ivy/cacti

贴心提示 Tips

室内花卉对人身体有好处的多为绿叶植物，比如绿萝、仙人球等。

Vine plants like ivy may be beneficial for people's health.

我自己拿。
Wǒ zìjǐ ná.
I'll take it myself.

147

对话 Dialogue

A:给您这花。

　Gěi nín zhè huā.　Here is your flower.

B:我自己拿。

　Wǒ zìjǐ ná.　I'll take it myself.

类似说法 Similar Expressions

我自己来。　I'll do it on my own.

反义 Antonym

我自己拿。—— 您帮我拿。　I'll take it myself. ——
Please help me to take it.

幽默 Humor

自己挑的才好看。　What I choose is the best looking.

联想 Association

鲜插花/盆花/盆景　cut fresh flower/potted flower/mini-
ascape

296

一般人买花,都喜欢自己挑选;所以,如果卖花人主动给您拿花,您可以说"我自己拿"。好多花市里面还有茶市、鱼市、小饰品店,您也可以顺便逛逛。您在花市里走累了,可以在茶市里喝喝茶,休息一会儿。喝茶时和茶老板聊聊天儿,他会告诉您很多有关茶的知识,也很有乐趣呢!

We usually choose flowers by ourselves. If the seller picks for you, you may say "I'll take it myself". In some of the flower markets there are also tea houses, fish stalls and accessories stores. You may go around and look at these too. If you are tired, you can sit in a tea house for a break. If you chat with the boss you may get to know many things about tea. It is a pleasure indeed!

148

要狗吗?
Yào gǒu ma?
Do you need a dog?

对话 Dialogue

A:要狗吗?
　Yào gǒu ma?　Do you need a dog?
B:看看。
　Kànkan.　I am just looking around.

类似说法 Similar Expressions

买狗吗?　Do you want a dog?

幽默 Humor

您要最忠实的朋友吗?　Do you want a most truthful friend?

联想 Association

猫/鸟/兔子/金鱼　cat/bird/rabbit/goldfish

现在狗市挺多,如果您喜欢狗,有空可以去逛逛;不一定买,随便看看也有乐趣。

Now there are lots of dog markets. If you like dogs, you may go to have a look.

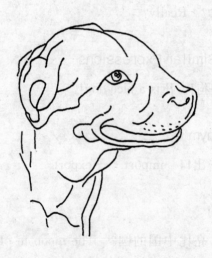

这狗是进口的!
Zhè gǒu shì jìnkǒu de!
The species of dog is not native to China!

对话 Dialogue

A：这狗是进口的!
Zhè gǒu shì jìnkǒu de!　The species of dog is not n-
ative to China!

B：是吗?
Shì ma?　Really?

类似说法 Similar Expressions

这可是好狗!　It is a nice dog!

反义 Antonym

进口——出口　import——export

幽默 Humor

外国的月亮比中国的圆?　The moon in other countries
looks brighter than in China?

联想 Association

贵妇狗/哈巴狗/狼狗/猎狗　Lady dog/Pekinese/demi-
wolf/courser

看看可以，可不要轻易买下来哦。

You may have a look, but do not make a hasty decision to buy a dog.

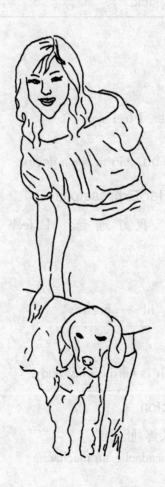

看病
kàn bìng **Seeing a Doctor**

我病了。
Wǒ bìng le.
I feel sick.

对话 Dialogue

A：我病了。

　　Wǒ bìng le. I feel sick.

B：去医院吧。

　　Qù yīyuàn ba. Go to see a doctor.

类似说法 Similar Expressions

我不舒服。/我好难受。 I feel uncomfortable. /I feel bad.

反义 Antonym

病——健康 ill——healthy

幽默 Humor

玉体欠安。 It is hard on my body.

联想 Association

感冒/咳嗽/头疼/肚子疼
cold/cough/headache/stomachache

302

北京有很多医院,小病可就近就医,大病可以去有名气的大医院。一般出租车司机或宾馆服务员都可以告诉您可去哪家医院。这里也为您提供几家大医院:友谊(综合性)、协和(综合性)、同仁(眼科最有名)、阜外(心血管)、积水潭(骨科)、中日友好(肿瘤)、北京大学第三临床医学院(产科、骨科、运动医学)。

There are many big hospitals in Beijing. For a minor illness you may go to the closest clinic and for big problem you may go to the well-known big hospitals. Taxi drivers or hotel attendants can tell you which hospital you should go to. The following lists some of the big ones: Consonancy Hospital (a medical complex), Tongren Hospital (specializing in Ophthalmology), Fuwai Hospital (Cardiovasular problems), Jishuitan Hospital (Osteology), Friendship Hospital (a medical complex), China-Japan Friendship Hospital (Oncology), The 3rd Hospital of Beijing University (Obstetrics, Osteology, Sports Medicine).

151

挂哪科?
Guà nǎ kē?
Which department do you need to visit?

对话 Dialogue

A:挂哪科?
Guà nǎ kē? Which department do you need to visit?
B:内科。
Nèi kē. Internal.

类似说法 Similar Expressions

挂什么科? /看哪科? What to register for? / Which department?

反义 Antonym

内科——外科 internal——surgery

幽默 Humor

治腰疼的那个科。 I want the department which can cure my waist pain.

联想 Association

外科/妇科/儿科/眼科/牙科/耳鼻喉科/传染科/中医科/专家号 Department of Surgery/Gynecology/Paediatrics/Ophthaulmology/Dentistry/Otorhinolaryngology/Infectious Disease/Traditional Chinese Medicine/Expert Registration

大型医院的分科都比较细,一般挂号处的护士会告诉您该挂哪科。您也可以多花点钱挂个专家号,听听专家的意见。

The departments in big hospitals are very clearly divided. The nurse in the Registrar's Office can tell you which department you should visit. You may also spend more money to register for an expert and get diagnosed by him/her.

152

肚子疼。
Dùzi téng.
I've got a stomachache.

Dialogue

A：您哪儿不舒服？
　　Nín nǎr bù shūfu?　Where is the discomfort?
B：肚子疼。
　　Dùzi téng.　I've got a stomachache.

类似说法 Similar Expressions

肚子不舒服。/肚子发痛。/肚子胀。
My stomach is uncomfortable. / I've got an abdominal
pain. / My stomach is swollen.

反义 Antonym

疼——不疼　painful——not painful

幽默 Humor

要生了。　You are going to give birth.

联想 Association

肠胃炎/饮食不卫生/吃多了　gastroenteritis/eat bad
food/eat too much

306

夏秋季节是肠胃病多发季节。北京小吃闻名中外,且荟萃了中国各地饮食。您一定要注意饮食卫生,尽量不在小摊上吃东西。

Gastroenteritis often happens in summer and autumn. Although Beijing has a variety of snacks and cuisines from other places, it is often hazardous to eat food prepared in small stalls.

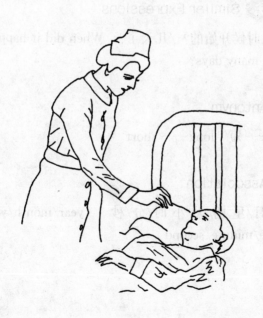

多长时间了？
Duō cháng shíjiān le?
How long did it last?

153

对话 Dialogue

A: 多长时间了？
   Duō cháng shíjiān le?   How long did it last?
B: 有半天了。
   Yǒu bàn tiān le.   Half a day.

类似说法 Similar Expressions

什么时候开始的？/几天了？   When did it happen? /For
how many days?

反义 Antonym

长——短   long——short

联想 Association

年/月/星 期/天/小 时/分/秒   year/month/week/day/
houe/minute/second

中国有句古话："病要早治，饭要热吃。"出门在外，一定要注意身体，有不舒服的地方及早去看医生。北京有较为发达的医疗机构，看病十分方便。

There is an old Chinese saying that says a disease is easy to cure at its beginning just as meals should be eaten when they are first served. When you are traveling, please take good care of your health. Go to see a doctor immediately whenever you feel ill. Beijing has a system of advanced medical care that can provide a prompt cure to most problems.

154

拉肚子了吗？
Lā dùzi le ma?
Do you have diarrhea?

对话 Dialogue

A: 拉肚子了吗？
　Lā dùzi le ma?　Do you have diarrhea?
B: 拉了两次。
　Lā le liǎng cì.　Yes, twice.

类似说法 Similar Expressions

大便多吗？/拉稀了吗？　How often have your bowels moved? / Do you have loose bowels?

反义 Antonym

拉肚子——便秘　diarrhea——constipation

幽默 Humor

跑肚了。　I am running to relieve myself.

　　中国传统医学讲究"望、闻、问、切"，为此，中医大夫会问病人比较多的情况，您可要尽量配合哟。

Traditional Chinese Medicine is famous for "Seeing, smelling, asking and feeling". Thus doctors tend to ask many questions. You should answer as accurately as possible.

155

吃什么了?
Chī shénme le?
What did you eat?

对话 Dialogue

    A：吃什么了?

      Chī shénme le?　What did you eat?

    B：吃了海鲜。

      Chī le hǎixiān.　Seafood.

类似说法 Similar Expressions

    吃什么东西了? /着凉了吗?　What did you eat? / Did you catch cold?

反义 Antonym

    吃——吐　eat——vomit

幽默 Humor

    什么都吃了。　I have eaten everything.

联想 Association

    鱼/虾/螃蟹/蛏子　fish/shrimp/crab/razor clam

在中国,"您吃了吗"一度是见面时的问候语,"吃什么"当然也是大家所关注的问题。不过在这里,大夫是想了解你是否吃过什么不卫生或不易消化的食物。

In China there was a popular phrase used as a greeting, "Have you eaten yet?" People are always interested in food. In this case the doctor just wants to know if the patient has eaten anything unhealthy or difficult to digest.

多喝开水。
Duō hē kāishuǐ.
Drink more hot water.

156

对话 Dialogue

A：多喝开水。

　　Duō hē kāishuǐ. Drink more hot water.

B：好的。

　　Hǎo de. Okay.

类似说法 Similar Expressions

勤喝水。 Drink water more frequently.

反义 Antonym

开水——生水 boiled water——tap water

幽默 Humor

白开水是最好的药。 Pure water is the best medicine.

联想 Association

凉水/生水 cold water/tap water

贴心提示 Tips

通常人生病的时候需要补充水分,所以多喝开水是最好的治疗。

When people are ill, it is often necessary to drink more water. Drinking water is often the best cure.

好好休息。
Hǎohǎo xiūxi.
Take a good rest

157

对话 Dialogue

A:好好休息。
Hǎohǎo xiūxi. Take a good rest.
B:是。
Shì. I will.

类似说法 Similar Expressions

多睡觉。 Sleep more

反义 Antonym

休息——工作/活动 rest——work/move

幽默 Humor

不会休息就不会工作。 No rest no work.

联想 Association

放松/静养/换换空气/泡个澡 relax/convalesce/take a breath/take a bath

316

生了病就别再坚持工作了。请几天病假，好好休息休息。

Do not continue to work while you are ill. Ask for some days off to have a good rest.

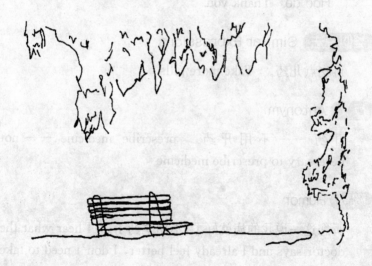

给您开点儿药。

Gěi nín kāi diǎnr yào.

I am prescribing some pills for you.

给您开点儿药。
Gěi nín kāi diǎnr yào.
I am prescribing some pills for you.

对话 Dialogue

A:给您开点儿药。

Gěi nín kāi diǎnr yào. I am prescribing some pills for you.

B:好的。

Hǎo de. Thank you.

类似说法 Similar Expressions

再吃点儿药。 Take more pills.

反义 Antonym

开药 —— 不用开药 prescribe medicine —— not necessary to prescribe medicine

幽默 Humor

听您这一说我的病就好了,不用吃药了。 I hear what the doctor says and I already feel better, I don't need to take any medicine.

联想 Association

打针/吃药/西药/中药 give an injection/take medicine/western medicine/traditional Chinese medicine

318

其实去医院不一定要拿药，有的病多喝水、多睡觉，不吃药也就好了。大夫的话有时很解决病人的思想负担。

In fact, it is not always necessary to buy medicine in the hospital. Drinking more water and sleeping more is often enough for people to recover from some minor diseases. Sometimes doctors function more like psychologists, relieving the patients' anxieties about their health.

159

给您处方。

Gěi nín chǔfāng.

Here is your prescription

Dialogue

A: 给您处方。

Gěi nín chǔfāng. Here is your prescription.

B: 60 块。

Liùshí kuài. 60 yuan.

类似说法 Similar Expressions

给您化验单。/给您预约单。/请划价。 Here are your test results. / Here is your booking slip. / Please give me the bill.

联想 Association

化验单/预约单/收据 test results/booking slip/receipt

320

中国大陆的医院一般是医、药合一的，医院又开处方又卖药。在北京的医院看病，先要挂号，然后到指定诊室看病，看完后拿着医生开的处方到收费处划价、交费，最后再到药房拿药。做各种化验、检查也是如此。明白这套程序，您可以省去许多麻烦。

Hospitals in mainland China diagnose illness and also sell medicine, that is, they will give prescriptions and sell the medicines. When seeing a doctor in Beijing, one must register first, then go to the designated room to meet the doctor, then go to pay the bill after getting the prescription and lastly, you may pick up the medicine from the Pharmacy. When having some tests or an examination done, you need to follow the same procedure. If you read this tip, you may save a lot of time.

160

有中医吗?
Yǒu zhōngyī ma?
Do you have a herbalist doctor?

对话 Dialogue

A：有中医吗？
Yǒu zhōngyī ma?　Do you have a herbalist doctor?
B：有。
Yǒu.　Yes, we do.

类似说法 Similar Expressions

可以看中医吗？/挂中医科。　May I see a traditional Chinese doctor? /register for the department of traditional Chinese medicne

反义 Antonym

中医 —— 西医　traditional Chinese doctor —— western doctor

幽默 Humor

我一见西药就头疼。/我一听打针就想跑。
I get a headache when seeing western medicine and want to run when being injected.

联想 Association

汤药/丸药/针灸/号脉　medicial tea/pill/acupuncture/feel the pulse

322

既然到了中国,建议您不妨去看看中医。请老中医给您号号脉,看看舌苔,听听他对您身体的诊断,是不是符合实际,也是很有意思的。俗话说,心诚则灵嘛。

Since you are already in China, we suggest that you go to see a traditional Chinese doctor in case you are ill. It is an interesting experience to have an old Chinese doctor feel your pulse.

求 助
qiú zhù Asking for Help

161 北京大学电话多少?
Běijīng Dàxué diànhuà duōshǎo?
What is the phone number of Peking University?

 对话 Dialogue

A:北京大学电话多少?
Běijīng Dàxué diànhuà duōshǎo? What is the phone number of Peking University?

B:问 114。
Wèn yāo yāo sì. Dial 114.

类似说法 Similar Expressions

请问北京大学的电话号码? Would you please tell me the phone number of Peking University?

反义 Antonym

多——少 much——little

幽默 Humor

我想找北京大学聊天儿。 I'd like to talk with Peking University.

联想 Association

清华大学/人民大学/师范大学/体育大学/邮电大学
Qinghua University/People's Univeristy/Normal Univeristy/Sport University/University of Posts and Telecommunications

中国内地电话号码查询非常方便快捷,只要您拨打114,说明您要查的单位名称就可以了。如果要查外省市电话号码,在114前加拨该地区长途区号即可。

To inquire about a telephone number in mainland China, you can simply dial 114 and give the name of the company. If you are asking about a phone number in another province or municipality, you need to add the long distance code of that area before dialing 114.

162

明天天气怎么样?
Míngtiān tiānqì zěnmeyàng?
How is the weather tomorrow?

对话 Dialogue

A: 明天天气怎么样?
Míngtiān tiānqì zěnmeyàng? How is the weather to-morrow?

B: 看看晚报。
Kànkan wǎnbào. Let's see the evening newspaper.

类似说法 Similar Expressions

明天天气预报怎么样? What is the weather forecast for tomorrow?

反义 Antonym

明天——昨天 tomorrow——yesterday

幽默 Humor

老天爷脾气好吗? Does the god of weather have a good temper?

联想 Association

阴/晴/刮风/风力/风向/下雨/下雪/雾 overcast/fine/wind/wind power/wind direction/rain/snow/fog

326

贴心提示 Tips

北京四季分明,春夏两季气候都十分宜人。不过为保险起见,出行前您最好关注一下天气预报。除报纸、电视、广播外,您可以拨打声讯服务电话12121。另外也可以咨询当地人,北京人喜欢谈论天气,或许能给您提好的建议。

The four seasons of Beijing are distinctly recognizable. Spring and autumn are the best time of the year. To ensure suitable weather for going out, you'd better listen to the weather forecast. Besides reading the newspapers, or listening to TV and radio broadcasts, you can also dial 12121—the weather forecast number—to get information. Asking local people is another way to find out about the weather. Beijing citizens like to talk about the weather and they often give you good advice about it too.

着火了!
Zháohuǒ le!
It's on fire!

对话 Dialogue

A:着火了!
　Zháohuǒ le!　It's on fire!
B:快救火!
　Kuài jiùhuǒ!　Let's put it out!

类似说法 Similar Expressions

厨房冒烟了! /失火了!　There is smoke in the kitch-en! /It catches on fire!

反义 Antonym

着——灭　get——go out

幽默 Humor

火神爷来了!　The Fire God is coming!

联想 Association

消防队/灭火器/消防栓/自救/逃生　firehouse/fire extin-guisher/fire hydrant/save oneself/ flee for your life

近年来各级政府都十分重视消防工作,但火灾隐患依旧存在。万一遇到火情,您要尽可能在第一时间拨打 119 火警电话,保持冷静,做好自救、逃生。

Although these days, all levels of the government pay great attention to preventing fires, fires can not be totally avoided. In case of fire, please dial 119 first, this is fire department emergency number. Remember to remain calm and save your own life.

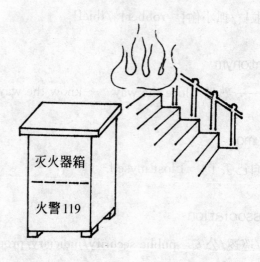

164

我迷路了!
Wǒ mílù le!
I lost my way!

对话 Dialogue

A:我迷路了!
Wǒ mílù le!　I lost my way!
B:找警察。
Zhǎo jǐngchá.　Ask the policeman!

类似说法 Similar Expressions

打劫啦! /抓小偷!　robber! /thief!

反义 Antonym

迷路——熟悉　lose the way——know the way

幽默 Humor

我把自己丢了。　I lost myself.

联想 Association

民警/巡逻/公安　public security/judiciary/procuratorate

"有困难找民警",这是人们共同的认识。当您碰到困难时,您可以请人民警察帮忙。在十字路口有交通警察,在公安的巡逻车里有巡警。如果周围找不到警察,您还可以拨打110报警,警察会在第一时间给您帮助。

"Please ask a policeman for help in case of an emergency." This is a common understanding. When you are experiencing some difficulty, a policemen can help you out. Traffic cops are on the crossroads and there are patrol cars on the streets. You may also dial 110 if you feel that you are in danger.

165

他休克了！
Tā xiūkè le!
He lost consciousness!

对话 Dialogue

A: 他休克了！
　　Tā xiūkè le!　He lost consciousness!
B: 快叫救护车！
　　Kuài jiào jiùhù chē!　Call for the ambulance.

类似说法 Similar Expressions

他昏过去了！　He is in a coma.

反义 Antonym

休克——清醒　lose consciousness——regain conscious-ness

幽默 Humor

他躺倒不干了。　He is not doing anything now.

联想 Association

中暑/犯病/车祸　heat stroke/to get ill/traffic accident

大城市的医疗急救很方便,遇到紧急情况需要医疗帮助时,您可以拨打120急救电话。

Big cities can provide convenient emergency medical treatment. You may dial the first aid number 120 or 999 in the event of a medical emergency.

166

我要寄东西。
Wǒ yào jì dōngxi.
I want to mail something.

对话 Dialogue

A:我要寄东西。

　　Wǒ yào jì dōngxi. I want to mail something.

B:去邮局。

　　Qù yóujú. Go to the Post Office.

类似说法 Similar Expressions

我寄包裹。 I want to post a parcel.

反义 Antonym

寄——不寄 post——do not post

幽默 Humor

我想把自己寄走。 I'd like to mail myself.

联想 Association

信件/包裹/挂号/汇款/特快专递
letter/parcel/registered/remittance/express mail

当您需要寄包裹、汇款、办理特快专递时,既可以到邮局直接办理,也可以打电话 11185 要求提供上门服务。各级邮政系统会给您提供优质的服务。

When you want to mail a parcel, send a remittance, or express mail something, you should go to the Post Office or dial 11185 to have the postal service come to your door. The Postal System in China will provide you with good services.

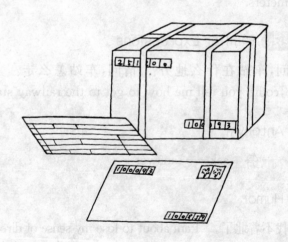

请问,火车站在哪儿?
Qǐngwèn, huǒchēzhàn zài nǎr?
Excuse me, could you tell me where the railway station is?

对话 Dialogue

A:请问,火车站在哪儿?

Qǐngwèn, huǒchēzhàn zài nǎr? Excuse me, could you tell me where the railway station is?

B:往前走 100 米。

Wǎng qián zǒu yìbǎi mǐ. Go straight ahead for 100 meters.

类似说法 Similar Expressions

请问,车站在什么地方? /请问,车站怎么走? Excuse me, could you tell me how to get to the railway station?

反义 Antonym

问——答 ask——answer

幽默 Humor

我找不着北了。 I am about to lose my sense of direction.

联想 Association

公共汽车站/机场/码头 bus stop/airport/wharf（or dock）

336

老百姓都很热情,愿意为您指路。但有的城市很大,不一定每个人都熟悉,您可以多问几个人,一般会得到满意的答案。

旅行前,您最好先买好火车票或飞机票。一般宾馆都有代售服务,您可以到服务台咨询,也可电话咨询。当然,您也可以亲自到分布在大街小巷的车票、机票代售处去买票,非常方便。

买票时,一定要选择好车次、航班。您可以提前上网或电话查询,也可以现场向售票人员咨询,搞清出发和到达时间,以便安排好自己的旅行。

Ordinary people are usually warm-hearted enough to answer questions about directions, but they may not know where everything is in such a large city. You may have to ask a number of people before you get a satisfactory answer.

You are advised to buy your tickets in advance. Many hotels provide services to help you purchase train and airplane tickets. You may consult the Information Desk or call them to ask about it. It is also convenient to buy tickets through many Ticket Agents that can be found everywhere.

Be sure to check the departure and arrival times of your train or flight. You may track it on internet or by telephone, or ask the salespersons so as to facilitate your travel.

请问,哪儿有卫生间?

Qǐngwèn, nǎr yǒu wèishēngjiān?

Excuse me, can you tell me where I can wash my hands?

对话 Dialogue

A:请问,哪儿有卫生间?

　Qǐngwèn, nǎr yǒu wèishēngjiān? Excuse me, can you tell me where I can wash my hands?

B:往前,左边。

　Wǎng qián, zuǒ biān. Go straight ahead, to your left.

类似说法 Similar Expressions

请问,洗手间怎么走? Excuse me, how do I get to the toilet?

反义 Antonym

前——后 ahead——behind 左——右 left——right

幽默 Humor

放点儿水。 I'd like to relieve some water.

联想 Association

方便/解手/厕所/茅房 relieve nature/answer nature's call/toilet/lavatory

　　有人说看一个国家的文明程度,就看那里的厕所。不知道您对中国的厕所印象如何?

　　Some people say that toilet facilities represent the level of a nation's civilization. What do you think of the toilets in China?

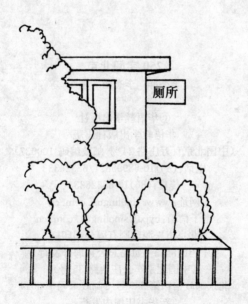

策　　划:单　瑛　责任编辑:龙燕俐　韩　晖　韩芙芸
封面设计:唐少文　印刷监制:佟汉冬

图书在版编目(CIP)数据

250字闯北京/李杰群主编.—北京:华语教学出版社,2005.7
ISBN 7-80200-099-8

Ⅰ. 2… Ⅱ. 李… Ⅲ. 汉语—口语 Ⅳ. H193.2

中国版本图书馆 CIP 数据核字(2005)第 065160 号

250 字闯北京

李杰群　李杰明　主编

*

ⓒ华语教学出版社

华语教学出版社出版

(中国北京百万庄路 24 号 邮政编码 100037)

电话:(86)10-68995871/68326333

传真:(86)10-68326333

网址:www.sinolingua.com.cn

电子信箱:hyjx@sinolingua.com.cn

北京市松源印刷有限公司印刷

中国国际图书贸易总公司海外发行

(中国北京车公庄西路 35 号)

北京邮政信箱第 399 号 邮政编码 100044

新华书店国内发行

2005 年(大 32 开)第一版

(汉英)

ISBN 7-80200-099-8

9-CE-3675P

定价:30.00 元